THE ILLINOIS LEGISLATURE

Structure and Process

Samuel K. Gove
Richard W. Carlson
Richard J. Carlson

Published for the
INSTITUTE OF GOVERNMENT AND PUBLIC AFFAIRS
by the
UNIVERSITY OF ILLINOIS PRESS
Urbana   Chicago   London

SPECIALISATION

LIBRARY OF CONGRESS CATALOGING IN PUBLICATION DATA

Gove, Samuel Kimball.
  The Illinois Legislature.

  Prior editions published under title: An introduction
to the Illinois General Assembly.
  Bibliography: p.
  Includes index.
  1.   Illinois.   General Assembly.   I.   Carlson,
Richard W., 1946-   joint author.   II.   Carlson,
Richard J., 1943-   joint author. III. Illinois. University at
Urbana-Champaign.   Institute of Government and Public
Affairs.   IV.   Title.
JK5766.G68   1976   328.773   76-21238
ISBN 0-252-00446-7 pbk.

Contents

Timing

Explanation

TABLES

CHART

Preface

The Illinois General Assembly has undergone many changes in recent years. Illinois lawmakers have been playing a different game. The legislators themselves appear to be different from their counterparts ten or twenty years ago — as a group they are younger, better educated, and harder workers. Their facilities and surroundings are greatly improved, as are their perquisites. The Illinois legislature is quite well-staffed now — at least compared to ten years ago, when research and technical staff was nonexistent. The impact of these changes on the public policies of the state is debatable; certainly this impact is not readily quantifiable.

The changes in Illinois are in line with national trends to strengthen the state legislative institution. The developments in Illinois have been looked upon favorably by persons outside the state. In fact, as early as 1971, the Citizens Conference on State Legislatures ranked Illinois as having the third best legislature in the nation. This ranking would probably still be the same (if not higher) if another survey were made using the same criteria.

This book describes the Illinois General Assembly — its structure, its processes — to give the interested citizen, the student, and indeed the public official (including the legislator), a better understanding of this very complex and important legislative body. We do not attempt to discuss the legislative product, but we do try to describe the legislature's relations with other aspects of the Illinois governmental structure. Another caution: we do not necessarily think that all is well with the legislative system, but our self-designated role is not to suggest reorganization or reforms. We leave this to others. Possibly our information and data will be helpful to those who do want to revise the process.

The Illinois Legislature: Structure and Process grew out of a grant given in 1968 by the American Political Science Association to the senior author. Based on that grant and resulting activity, a multilithed monograph, *An Introduction to the Illinois General Assembly,* was prepared primarily for new members of the legislature in 1968. The monograph was also built upon several editions of "Lawmaking in the Illinois General Assembly," first published by the Illinois Legislative Council in 1960. In 1970, 1972, and 1974 the *Introduction* was given three major revisions. There were many reasons why changes in the monograph were necessary. One not unimportant reason was the new 1970 Illinois Constitution. Others are mentioned frequently in the body of the manuscript.

Because of the many revisions made in the earlier monographs we felt that the material was ready for further revision and dissemination in a more permanent form. Thus this book. But we should hasten to say we expect many more changes in future years. In regard to the present work, we used January 1976 as the cutoff point for material and data.

As for any undertaking of this kind, many acknowledgments are in order. The financial support of the American Political Science Association is appreciated, as is that of the Illinois Legislative Council through its two recent research directors, William Day and William Hey. Mentioning the somewhat confusing names of Day and Hey brings up the even more confusing situation of my coauthors. Both Richard Walter Carlson and Richard John Carlson have been graduate students of mine. Both were legislative interns in the period during which I served as program coordinator of the Illinois Legislative Internship Program. Fortunately, they answer to the names of Rick and Rich respectively. Richard W. Carlson is now on the staff of the state Senate in Springfield; Richard J. Carlson is director of research for the Council of State Governments in Lexington, Kentucky. The latter worked on the first edition of the *Introduction;* the former on three extensive revisions, including this manuscript. Ashley Nugent and James Schratz helped with the 1970 edition.

Several staff members of the Institute of Government and Public Affairs, University of Illinois, made valuable contributions. These include the skillful editorial work of Ashley Nugent and Stephanie Cole and the critical secretarial help of the Institute secretary, Jean Baker. Particularly helpful was Professor Jack Isakoff of Southern Illinois University, Carbondale. There are others too numerous to mention, including the several anonymous legislators who were helpful; some of them are quoted in the book.

As always, the authors take responsibility for any errors of commission or omission.

SAMUEL K. GOVE
Director, Institute of Government and Public Affairs

1

The General Assembly as Agent of the People

Most, if not all, of the prevailing political interests in Illinois re-emerge with the convening of each session of the General Assembly. At least once each year there is a mass influx of lobbyists, reporters, and politically interested citizens into the state's capital city. There is, in fact, no other activity which swells the population, the economy, even the pace of life in Springfield as much. Why all this excitement and turmoil? Probably because those who follow the Illinois General Assembly have learned that when the legislature is not itself initiating a change in public policy, it can assert its power to check, frustrate, delay, reject, modify, or adopt the policy initiatives of the governor, the mayor of the city of Chicago, one of the other elected state officials, or various interest groups.

There are in Illinois 236 men and women with varying degrees of experience who have sought and won election by the people of one of the fifty-nine legislative districts. As the General Assembly, they assert their role in making the policy of state government. They review and evaluate the conduct of state administration and the effects of state programs. Even when they are not in the state capital, these legislators maintain contacts with and work for constituents, month in and month out. In the interim periods when the legislature is recessed, legislators are also kept busy by committees and commissions which continue to function during the entire biennium.

THE LEGISLATURE — FIRST AMONG COEQUALS

Symbolic of the legislature's critical role in state government is the "enacting clause," which Article IV, section 8(a), of the 1970 Illinois Constitution requires to appear in all bills that are to become law: "Be it enacted by the People of the State of Illinois, represented in the General Assembly." The significance of this enacting clause is twofold. First, on a theoretical level, it identifies the people as the ultimate source of law and the legislature as the agent of the people. Second, on a practical level, it illustrates the kind of detail that is still found in the new state constitution with regard to the legislative branch; a bill passed without this enacting clause would be without effect.

The state constitution (both the old and new) channels the power of the state into three branches — the legislative, the executive, and the judicial — and expressly prohibits any one branch from exercising powers allocated to either of the others. Although the lines separating each of the three branches of state government have never been completely clear, the essential responsibility of the General Assembly has always been that of enacting statute law (see the chart, "The Illinois Legislature," pp. 4-5).

Speaking of the crucial nature of this separation of powers which both our state and federal constitutions provide, and arguing the need for strong, resourceful legislatures, Larry Margolis, executive director of the Citizens Conference on State Legislatures (now Legis 50/The Center for Legislative Improvement), has said:

> The uniqueness of the American experiment in democracy — the gamble that our founding fathers took — lies in a system that does not intend to be the most efficient, but one in which there is a possibility of achieving effective government while preserving the greatest possible degree of personal freedom.
>
> To achieve both effective government and personal freedom, a rather complex system was devised that distributes power among units of government and among branches of government and pits them against one another. . . .
>
> If any of the elements in this intricately balanced and complex system is comparatively weak, the system does not work. In fact, it becomes dangerous. Imbalance in such a system can produce

paralysis, because while there is a sufficient distribution of power to prevent action, there is not enough capability to perform and to respond to challenges.[1]

The General Assembly, in both a constitutional and a democratic sense, represents all the people of Illinois. The elected legislators exercise the sovereign power of the state in the name of the people. This is the basis for some of the great powers vested in the legislature and for some aspects of its procedure.

CONSTITUTIONAL POWERS

Statute Law

Most enactments of the General Assembly become part of the statute law, as distinguished from such other standards of conduct as those inherited from English common law or formulated by present-day courts and local governments. These statutes may affect virtually every activity involving individuals, groups, and corporations in the state, a situation that has led to the enormous quantity of bills and resolutions that have been introduced in recent years. Although many involve fundamental matters usually only a few major bills command virtually all the media attention devoted to legislation. The bills of greatest concern to the general public usually involve revenue, appropriations, education, or judicial matters. No issue can be settled for all time, and, as William Keefe points out, each time a new law is added to the statutes, a strong possibility exists that subsequent general assemblies will be required to rework it through amendatory bills. "In a word," Keefe says, "law begets law."[2] A heavy proportion of all the bills introduced and adopted are of this nature. While they have general relevance for the system, they usually have only slight relevance for the public.

The governor shares in this lawmaking process at many stages, notably in his power either to recommend changes to the legisla-

[1] Larry Margolis, "Revitalizing State Legislatures," in *Strengthening the States: Essays on Legislative Reform*, ed. Donald Herzberg and Alan Rosenthal (Garden City, N.Y.: Doubleday, 1971), pp. 25-26.

[2] William J. Keefe, "The Functions and Powers of the State Legislature," in *State Legislatures in American Politics*, ed. Alexander Heard (Englewood Cliffs, N.J.: Prentice Hall, 1966), p. 40.

THE ILLINOIS LEGISLATURE

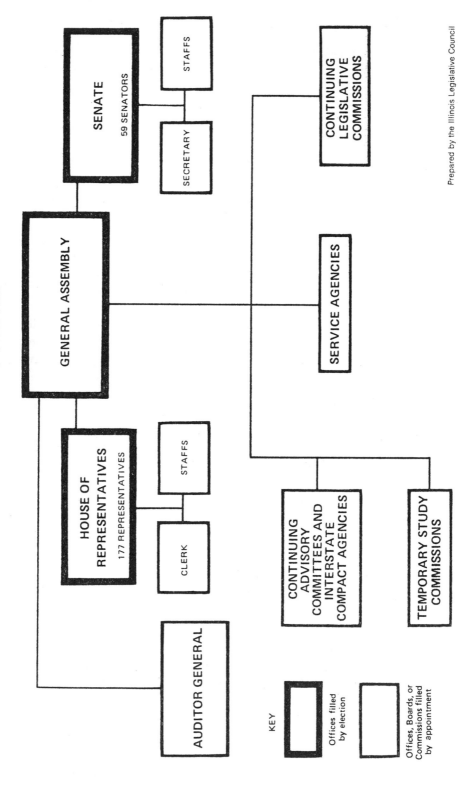

Prepared by the Illinois Legislative Council

CONTINUING LEGISLATIVE COMMISSIONS

Bicentennial
Bi-State Development District and Bi-State Development
Agency Visitation
Capitol City Planning
Children
Cities and Villages Municipal Problems
Council on Aging
County Problems
Data Information Systems
Economic Development
Election Laws
Energy Resources
General Assembly Retirement System Trustees
Labor Laws
Little Calumet River Flood Control Coordinating
Medical Injury Insurance Reparations
Mental Health and Developmental Disabilities
Motor Vehicle Laws
Pension Laws
Recreation Council
School Problems
Senate Operations
Spanish Speaking People
Special Events
Status of Women
Transportation Study
Visit and Examine State Institutions
Water Resources

SERVICE AGENCIES

Economic and Fiscal Commission
Makes state program evaluations and economic forecasts.

Intergovernmental Cooperation Commission
Compiles information on federal programs and provides intergovernmental liaison services.

Legislative Council
Conducts nonpartisan research and provides duplicating services for the General Assembly; sponsors legislative intern program and orientation conference for new members.

Legislative Information System Committee
Provides computer services to General Assembly.

Legislative Investigating Commission
Investigates matters of interest to the General Assembly.

Legislative Reference Bureau
Prepares bills and amendments and publishes digest of bills during sessions.

Legislative Space Needs
Allocates space in facilities used by the General Assembly and its agencies; reviews contracts for construction or repair of all state buildings in Capitol complex.

ture or to veto a bill, his authority to reorganize the executive branch of government subject to a legislative veto, and the long-standing tradition that the chief executive proposes his own legislative program.

State and Local Administration

The General Assembly by law establishes most of the administrative agencies of state government and prescribes their organization, duties, and procedures. Excepted from legislative control to a limited degree are those state offices mentioned in the constitution. The legislature cannot by statute abolish offices or impinge on responsibilities controlled by the constitution. Under the governor's new executive reorganization authority, if either house does not specifically reject an executive order by a majority vote on a roll call within sixty days of its receipt, that executive order will become effective.

If the executive order is delivered after April 1 or when the General Assembly is not in session, the General Assembly is to consider the reorganization plan at its next annual session. In that case, the executive order is constitutionally deemed to have been delivered on the first day of the later session thus giving the General Assembly sixty days from that day in which to act on the governor's proposal. Thus, if the governor submits a reorganization plan early in the session, the General Assembly will have only sixty days to veto the plan or watch it become effective with or without its approval. There is no legal obstacle, however, to the General Assembly giving these constitutionally created offices added duties or creating internal administrative units in them if this does not violate the intent of the constitution.

Oversight of the administration, Keefe reminds us, has long been regarded as an essential function of representative assemblies: "Just as no statute can settle a matter for all time, no language ... can guarantee that the policy will be administered as the legislature intended. If for no other reason, the legislature's self-interest demands that it oversee administration to learn whether agencies are complying with legislative intent."[3]

3 Ibid., p. 44.

The 1970 Illinois Constitution has a great deal more to say about local government than its predecessor did. With an entire article (Art. VII) devoted to local government, the new constitution covers county and township organization; powers of home rule units, non-home rule units, school districts, and other units of local government; salaries and fees; intergovernmental cooperation; and methods of changing local government structure and functions.

Home Rule

Under the new constitution, home rule units are not dependent on the General Assembly to enact legislation affecting their powers and functions. Qualifying for home rule status are those municipalities over 25,000 population, smaller municipalities which elect by referendum to become home rule units, and counties with an elected chief executive officer. (Currently Cook County is the only Illinois county in this category.) A home rule unit may also revert to its former non-home rule status by referendum.

With certain specific limitations, a home rule unit may "exercise any function pertaining to its government and affairs including, but not limited to, the power to regulate for the protection of the public health, safety, morals and welfare; to license; to tax; and to incur debt."

There are two kinds of specific limitations to this broad grant of power. The first group, spelled out in subsection 6(e) of Article VII, relates to limitations on the taxing power of home rule units. These local governments cannot (1) license for revenue, (2) impose taxes upon or measured by income or earnings, or (3) tax occupations, unless the legislature grants these powers. Writing after the constitution had been ratified, John Parkhurst, chairman of the constitutional convention's Local Government Committee, observed, "The more controversial kinds of local revenue-raising powers are precluded for home rule units, and left to the infinite wisdom of the General Assembly and to the unforeseeable vicissitudes of the future. The door is closed, but it is not locked."[4] The General As-

---

[4] John C. Parkhurst, "Two Years Later: The Status of Home Rule in Illinois," in *Home Rule in Illinois,* Final Report, Background Papers, and Speeches, Assembly on Home Rule in Illinois, ed. Stephanie Cole and Samuel K. Gove (Urbana: Institute of Government and Public Affairs, University of Illinois, 1973), p. 22.

sembly may deny or limit any other taxing power not specifically limited by subsection 6(e), but would have to do so by an extraordinary three-fifths majority vote of both houses. The taxing powers of home rule units are touched on somewhat further in the section below on revenue.

The "preemption" provisions of the new constitution, subsections (g), (h), and (i) of Article VII, section 6, constitute the second group of limitations on home rule powers. These subsections spell out the most important ways in which the legislature plays a role in Illinois home rule. An understanding of the differences between these three subsections is important for determining when the extraordinary three-fifths majority is required to approve individual pieces of legislation.

Subsection 6(g) provides for the denial or limitation by a three-fifths majority of both houses of the General Assembly of home rule powers in two areas. One of these is the power to tax, which has been discussed above. The other deals with state legislative preemption of "any other power or function of a home rule unit not exercised or performed by the State. . . ." A mere denial or limitation of a home rule power, as permitted by subsection (g), can again be enacted only by a three-fifths majority of both houses of the General Assembly. However, subsection (h) allows for preemption by a simple majority (a majority of the members elected to both houses) "when a state statute actually exercises a governmental power or authorizes a state agency to do so."[5] Parkhurst calls this "positive" preemption. Subsection 6(i) deals with the nonexclusive exercise of state power and provides for the state and home rule units to exercise their powers concurrently if the General Assembly "by law does not specifically limit the concurrent exercise or specifically declare the State's exercise to be exclusive."

Parkhurst has identified these three preemption subsections as the heart of the home rule concept in Illinois. Through them, he says, the convention threw the ball to the legislature to shape and control the evolution of the system and to resolve the conflicts.[6] The late Professor David C. Baum, who was the counsel for Parkhurst's

[5] Illinois, Sixth Constitutional Convention, *Record of Proceedings, Committee Proposals — Member Proposals* (Springfield, 1972), Local Government Committee Proposal 1, VII:1642.
[6] Parkhurst, "Two Years Later," p. 23.

committee at the convention, explained the intent of these sections this way: "The design of Section 6 places great responsibility upon the legislature to ensure that home rule does not degenerate into provincialism which could injure the people of the state. This emphasis on legislative authority to limit home rule, plus the specification of ways in which the legislature must act to assert its authority, makes the Illinois home rule provision unique."[7]

By the end of 1975 there were eighty-seven home rule municipalities in Illinois. Nineteen of these units, with populations under 25,000, had adopted home rule by referendum; nine municipal home rule referenda had been defeated. Cook County was the only home rule county. Nine other counties had tried to attain home rule by adopting the elected chief executive officer form of government by referendum; all were unsuccessful.[8]

Revenue

An important constitutional power of the General Assembly is to provide revenue for state and local governments. Property taxes and other taxes are levied on the basis of laws enacted by the legislature; they are then collected by local governments and by administrative agencies of the state. The constitution establishes certain principles of taxation while the legislature develops them into specific measures. In this way the General Assembly shapes the way monies are collected by all levels of Illinois government. This is a critically important power since the availability of fiscal resources often determines how government meets its responsibilities.

As discussed above, the 1970 constitution grants home rule units the power to tax and incur debt subject to certain limitations. For instance, a home rule unit cannot license for revenue unless the General Assembly should grant this right. The General Assembly by a three-fifths vote of each house may deny or limit the power of a home rule unit to tax.

The imposition of new or additional taxes to raise additional local revenue without legislative authorization has been one of the

[7] David C. Baum, "A Tentative Survey of Illinois Home Rule (Part I): Powers and Limitations," *University of Illinois Law Forum* 1972, no. 1, p. 157.
[8] See Stephanie Cole, "Home Rule in Illinois: No. 1. The Constitutional Provisions," *Illinois Issues* 1 (April 1975):104-8, and "Home Rule in Illinois: No. 4. Local Action," *Illinois Issues* 1 (August 1975):243-46.

main uses of these new home rule powers. Hotel and motel rooms, cigarettes, factories, and businesses have been taxed; municipal utility taxes as well as new parking taxes have been imposed. The city of Chicago in particular has made strong use of this authority, and the Illinois Supreme Court has thus far upheld its authority to impose among others a cigarette tax, a parking tax, a wheel tax, a transaction tax on the transfer of real property and the rental or leasing of personal property, and an employer's expense tax ("head tax"). Hotel and motel taxes have been imposed in Chicago as well as in several other suburban and downstate cities without any legal challenges.[9]

The legislature may, again with an extraordinary three-fifths majority, also limit the amount of debt a home rule municipality can incur without referendum. Such limitations, if enacted, can limit nonreferendum debt only when it exceeds a set percentage of the home rule municipality's total assessed valuation. Home rule county debt may be limited by simple majority vote of the legislature.

Otherwise, the incurring of debt by state and local governments is subject to legislative authorizations within new, less restrictive, constitutionally prescribed limits. Under the 1970 constitution, the General Assembly may, without a statewide referendum on the question, put the state's full faith and credit behind debt authorized by a three-fifths majority of each house. The impact of this change has already been profound. In the first three years under the new constitution, the General Assembly authorized four major general obligation bond issues totaling over $2.2 billion. This early trend appears certain to become an established pattern as each year brings new gubernatorial requests for major increases in bond authorizations. The referendum requirement of the old constitution restricted the use of this means of financing, and forced the state to finance its capital needs through the back door use of the Illinois Building Authority. Approximately $1.2 billion in state bonds was issued over twenty-five years as the result of successful referenda in 1946, 1960, and 1970 for veterans' bonuses, university buildings and mental health facility buildings, and antipollution programs, respectively. In addition to these bond issues there were only four other successful

[9] *Home Rule Newsletter* no. 7, Institute of Government and Public Affairs, University of Illinois, Urbana, May 1974, and Jerry DeMuth, "Home-Rule Power Used Mainly for Revenue," *Chicago Sun-Times*, May 26, 1974.

referenda (1918, 1922, 1932, 1934) during the life of the old constitution, which dated from 1870. Those were for highways, soldiers' bonuses, and twice for emergency relief.

Appropriations

Often referred to as the "power of the purse," it is through the appropriations process that the legislature arranges the priorities of state government and possesses the potential for controlling or restricting the administration of the executive branch.

The budget-making process in Illinois has undergone several significant changes since the publication of Thomas Anton's authoritative book on the subject.[10] The old Budgetary Commission has been abolished, and the Illinois Economic and Fiscal Commission has taken its place.[11] As part of the governor's office, the new state Bureau of the Budget is now totally responsible for preparation of what can be called a true executive budget. Constitutionally, the state budget must be prepared and presented to the General Assembly by the governor once a year. His budget must set forth an estimated balance of funds available for appropriation at the beginning of the fiscal year, an estimate of receipts, and a plan for expenditures and obligations during the fiscal year for every department, authority, public corporation, and quasi-public corporation of the state, every state college and university, and every other public agency created by the state except units of local government and school districts. The governor's budget must also set forth the indebtedness and contingent liabilities of the state and such other information as may be required by law. Finally, the 1970 constitution mandates that the governor's proposed expenditures not exceed his estimate of funds to be available for the coming year. Statute requires that this all be done on or before March 1.

The governor's budget document is then translated into appro-

[10] Thomas J. Anton, *The Politics of State Expenditure in Illinois* (Urbana: University of Illinois Press, 1966).

[11] Created by P.A. 77-2054, approved July 13, 1972, this bipartisan commission is a twenty-member body made up of the chairmen and minority spokesmen of the House and Senate appropriations and revenue committees, plus six other members from each house, three being appointed by each party's leader. Among the commission's enumerated statutory duties is the responsibility for developing an estimate of revenue likely to be available during the next fiscal year, which the General Assembly will adopt or modify as its estimate of revenue pursuant to Art. VIII, sec. 2(b), of the 1970 constitution.

priation bills which often spell out the purposes for which the money may be used by specifying both the internal organization of an agency and the type of operating expenditure (e.g., personal services) in separate line items. Legislation approved in 1973 requires that these bills be introduced no later than the first Friday in April, although this has not yet been strictly adhered to. Under the new constitution all expenditures of public funds, including most federal grants, must be appropriated by the General Assembly, and the sum of these appropriations for a given fiscal year must not exceed the legislature's own estimate of the funds that will be available during that year.[12]

In recent years legislative appropriations have also included an ever increasing amount of state support for local governmental functions. Prominent instances of such support are funds allotted for school and local road purposes and the state's no-strings-attached revenue-sharing program with counties and municipalities.[13]

All appropriation bills traverse the legislative process like other bills. Upon passage they become temporary parts of the body of statute law. Committee deliberations have become more important

[12] In September 1974 the Illinois Supreme Court noted the long-standing practice of expending some state funds without a current appropriation in ordering the payment of a voucher drawn against a federal trust fund, even though this would mean the expenditure of state funds without an appropriation. The state comptroller had refused to pay the voucher, citing this constitutional provision and a specific statutory prohibition in the appropriation bill involved. While declining to rule directly on the constitutional issue of whether all expenditures of public funds must come from appropriations made by the General Assembly, the court held that the language in the appropriation bill, which prohibited the expenditure of any federal funds received in excess of that appropriation without an additional appropriation, violated the constitutional provision limiting appropriation bills to the subject of appropriations. See *People ex rel. Kirk v. Lindberg*, 59 Ill. 2d 38, 320 N.E.2d 17 (1974).

[13] The 1972 Census of Governments revealed that in 1972 Illinois ranked fourth among the fifty states in the amount of state dollars returned to local governments; it ranked twenty-second in per capita support. Altogether over $1.6 billion of the state budget for that year was returned to the local level, up from $703 million in 1967. In terms of per capita support of local governments, Illinois rose from $64.56 in 1967 to $144.68 in 1972, which was the sixth largest percentage increase among the states. This brought Illinois above the median for the first time, after its thirty-sixth place ranking in 1967. The percentage distribution of Illinois's support of its local governments in 1972 was as follows: general local government support, 5.2 percent; education, 65.6 percent; highways, 12.2 percent; public welfare, 12.9 percent; miscellaneous, 4.1 percent. See U.S., Bureau of the Census, *Census of Governments, 1972*, vol. 6, *Topical Studies, No. 3: State Payments to Local Governments* (Washington, D.C.: U.S. Government Printing Office, 1974).

to the process with the addition of professional staff for both the majority and minority members of the Appropriations Committee in each chamber. Subcommittees and majority party task forces are now the scene of the intensive review and bargaining that formerly occurred in the Budgetary Commission. Their recommendations almost always prevail in their own chamber, and the members of these subgroups are usually their chamber's representatives in the many conference committees that often develop.

To return to William Keefe's discussion of legislative oversight, he notes: "Ordinarily, the best opportunity to review and influence administrative behavior occurs during the process of considering the governor's budget. At this point administrators can be asked to account for the performance of their agencies, to explain past expenditures, and to justify the funds requested for the new fiscal year."[14]

Postaudit Review of Expenditures

In another change brought about by the new state constitution, the General Assembly now appoints its own auditor general, who serves a ten-year term and is to audit, or cause to be audited, the obligation, receipt, and use of public funds of the state. The first legislative auditor general was confirmed by the required extraordinary majorities in both houses of the General Assembly after his appointment had been recommended by the Legislative Audit Commission; he assumed office on August 1, 1974.

This new legislative agency replaces the Department of Audits, which had been part of the executive branch, and is responsible for conducting a financial audit of each state agency at least once during every biennium. The auditor general works in cooperation with the Legislative Audit Commission, which may authorize him to conduct either a management or program audit of a state agency. The Audit Commission may authorize the auditor general to make certain investigations, which may be recommended by the auditor general or by the commission membership. The auditor general also has jurisdiction over local government agencies and private agencies as to the use of state funds which were granted with specific limita-

[14] Keefe, "The Functions and Powers," p. 45.

tions or conditions imposed by law. Finally, the auditor general may initiate and conduct an efficiency audit of any state agency or program whenever the findings of a postaudit indicate that such an audit is advisable if, after thirty days' notice, the Audit Commission has not disapproved of that audit.

A nonpartisan appointee, the auditor general is required by law to abstain from any political activity. The law also imposes limitations designed to assure his impartiality. Patterned after the General Accounting Office which serves the U.S. Congress, this new office is an important and powerful arm of the General Assembly.

Constitutional Changes

The General Assembly is also responsible for initiating changes in the state constitution although the current charter provides alternative methods for change should the General Assembly not act.[15]

The question of whether to call a constitutional convention to consider reworking the document as a whole can be submitted to the voters at any general election, provided at least three-fifths of the members elected to each house approve an enabling resolution at least six months prior to the election. If a convention call is approved by three-fifths of those voting on the question or a majority of those voting in the election, the legislature must then provide by law for the election, meeting, and expenses of the convention. Any proposed revision of or amendments to the constitution approved by a majority of the convention delegates elected must then be submitted to the electorate, with a majority of those voting on the question required for ratification.

The state's present constitution is the product of Illinois's Sixth Constitutional Convention, which convened in Springfield on December 8, 1969, and adjourned on September 3, 1970. The new constitution was ratified by nearly 56 percent of those voting in a special election held December 15, 1970. Most of its provisions became effective July 1, 1971.

Specific amendments to the constitution may be proposed by the General Assembly directly, again by a three-fifths vote of the mem-

---

[15] See the discussion below on constitutional provisions for an automatic referendum every twenty years on whether to call a constitutional convention, and for an initiative and referendum on structural or procedural changes in the legislative article.

bers elected to each house. Any such proposed amendment goes into effect if, at the general election next occurring at least six months after such legislative initiative, the amendment is approved by either three-fifths of those voting on the question or a majority of those voting in the election. However, the General Assembly may submit proposals to amend no more than three articles of the constitution at any one time, and no amendment may be proposed or submitted by the legislature from the time a convention is called until after the electors have voted on the revision or amendments, if any, proposed by the convention.

In addition to the governor's executive reorganization authority discussed above, the 1970 constitution provides several changes that have the effect of allowing the initiative for certain changes to come from outside the legislature. Private citizens can by petition initiate a referendum on changes in structural and procedural subjects in the legislative article (IV) of the constitution if 8 percent of the vote cast in the preceding gubernatorial election is obtained on such petitions. The petitions must be signed not more than twenty-four months preceding the general election at which the proposed amendment is submitted, and must be filed together with the text of the proposed amendment with the secretary of state at least six months before that general election. If the petitions are judged to be valid and sufficient, the proposed amendment will be placed before the voters at the next general election. To become effective the amendment must be approved by either three-fifths of those voting on the amendment or a majority of those voting in the election.

Constitutional change without legislative action may occur in yet another way: the question of whether to call a constitutional convention must automatically appear on the ballot at the general election in the twentieth year following the last submission. Thus the electorate will be voting on a constitutional convention call at least once every twenty years regardless of what action the General Assembly does or does not take.

The General Assembly may be called upon by the Congress to consider amendments to the federal Constitution, for ratification either by legislatures or by conventions in the several states. The new Illinois Constitution requires the affirmative vote of three-fifths of the members elected to each house for the General Assembly to petition Congress to call a federal constitutional convention, to ratify a proposed amendment to the U.S. Constitution, or to call a state convention to ratify a proposed amendment to the federal Constitution.[16]

Investigations

Although bill consideration may involve questioning or testimony in the nature of an inquiry, the General Assembly conducts investigations of governmental or other matters only on a limited basis. But it has general power to make investigations appropriate to the legislative function, and on occasion a special inquiry is authorized. Perhaps one of the more common of these relates to contested elections to the General Assembly. Since each house has complete constitutional discretion in determining the qualifications of its members, election disputes in Illinois have not been settled in court but by the chamber involved.[17] Inquiries into how state and local governments conduct their affairs are also possible, and even the behavior of private persons or business may have a sufficient relation to existing or needed legislation to permit detailed inquiries.

The distinguishing feature of an investigation is probably the power to compel by subpoena both the attendance and testimony of witnesses and the production of books, records, and papers. As provided in Article IV, section 7(c), of the state constitution, this power may be exercised by either house of the General Assembly,

[16] In a 1975 decision the United States District Court for the Northern District of Illinois held that the delegated federal power to state legislatures to ratify proposed amendments to the U.S. Constitution may not be inhibited by state constitutional provisions. The court also held, however, that the question of whether more than a simple majority vote is required to pass a ratifying resolution may be decided by each state legislature for itself. The additional requirement in the Illinois Constitution that a majority of the members of the General Assembly be elected after a proposed amendment has been submitted for ratification was invalidated in the same decision. See *Dyer* v. *Blair,* 390 F. Supp. 1291 (1975).

[17] Although each house is usually said to be the sole judge of the qualifications of its members, the U.S. Supreme Court has held that a state legislature is limited by certain federal constitutional standards in its right to judge its members. See *Bond* v. *Floyd,* 87 S.Ct. 339, 385 U.S. 116, 17 L.Ed. 2d 235 (1966). Thus, it is doubtful whether either house could exclude a person from its membership for reasons other than failure to comply with the constitutional requirements for holding a legislative office. Compare *Powell* v. *McCormack,* 89 S.Ct. 1944, 395 U.S. 486, 23 L.Ed. 2d 491 (1969), and *Reif* v. *Barrett,* 355 Ill. 104, 188 N.E. 889 (1934).

or any committee thereof.[18] Statutes allow these bodies to administer oaths and otherwise search out desired information rather than be content with what is offered as volunteered information, arguments, and answers to questions. During its 1971 session, the General Assembly established by law the Illinois Legislative Investigating Commission, which is empowered to conduct any investigation authorized by statute or established by a specific resolution of either or both houses of the General Assembly. A 1957 statute sets down various procedural requirements designed to protect the rights of those affected by any investigative hearings conducted apart from the operations of the legislature's standing committees.

Confirmation of Appointments

The Senate alone is given the power by the constitution of "advice and consent" to gubernatorial appointments to a number of state administrative offices. The Senate must act within sixty session days of its receipt of a nomination, and a majority of all the elected senators is necessary for confirmation.

Subject to confirmation, according to the constitution, are "all officers whose election or appointment is not otherwise provided for." Under existing laws this entails a long list ranging from department heads directly subordinate to the governor to nonsalaried members of various local and regional boards and commissions. In recent years the Senate has begun expending more time and resources on this function with the upper chamber now being in recess for no longer than about four months at any time. Prior to annual sessions a department director could have served for over eighteen months without coming up for Senate confirmation. While the events of recent years might be peculiar to the particular governor and senate involved, it appears that the result of these changes is going to be that the Senate will no longer confirm a gubernatorial nominee solely on the old principle that the governor is entitled to get whomever he wants for the job regardless of his qualifications. If con-

---

[18] In May 1974 an Illinois appellate court ruled that standing committees of the General Assembly do not have "the authority and power to conduct legislative investigations." This power, the court ruled, lies solely with the House and the Senate and must be transferred specifically by a bill or resolution to any committee or subcommittee. See *Murphy v. Collins,* 20 Ill. App. 3d 181, 312 N.E.2d 772 (1974). Leave to appeal to the Illinois Supreme Court was later denied.

tinued, this practice will certainly increase the importance of this particular Senate function.

Impeachment

The legislature may remove executive and judicial officers from office, an extreme action that is seldom taken. As Keefe observes, "In practical terms, the impeachment power is of scant significance and is seldom used. It is scarcely more appropriate for legislative control of administration than is Russian roulette for assuaging boredom — both neglect, and possibly forfeit, intermediate applications."[19] Such action can be threatened, however, as in 1974, when a resolution seeking the impeachment of a code department director "for failure to enforce the . . . law" was introduced in the House. The political atmosphere following the Watergate scandal and Richard Nixon's resignation of the presidency in the face of almost certain impeachment could result in more such resolutions being introduced. Prior to Watergate the use of the impeachment power was almost unheard of in Illinois.

Educating the Public

The most easily overlooked function of the legislature is that of informing and instructing the public. The business of the legislature on the floor and in committee is carried out in full public view to develop the dialogue essential to popular government. Floor debate and committee investigations are vital in stimulating the people's awareness of major public issues, and the Illinois General Assembly has been in the forefront among the nation's state legislatures in opening both its floor sessions and committee deliberations to the public. In accordance with both the state constitution and legislative rules, all legislative committees and commissions are required to give public notice of their meetings at least six days in advance.

CONSTITUTIONAL LIMITATIONS

Commenting on how most state constitutions severely limit the legislature's power to cope with many of the problems confronting state government today, William Keefe points out that:

[19] Keefe, "The Functions and Powers," p. 45.

Legislative creativity in the states, when and where it is found, exists despite the ideology and provisions of state constitutions. Without apparent exception, state constitutions in 1966 cast a net of suspicion over the legislature by circumscribing or limiting its powers and by making it difficult for state government to keep pace with the ideas and forms of mid-twentieth century America. . . .

. . . Many complaints concerning constitutional limitations converge on the central issue of the legislature's power over state finances. By any standard, the limitations imposed on the legislature are harsh.[20]

The 1970 Illinois Constitution does provide the General Assembly with considerably fewer restrictions than did the 1870 version. Gone are the extremely restrictive provisions for incurring state debt and the prohibitions against lotteries and changes in the general banking statutes. Sovereign immunity has been abolished. A laundry list of prohibitions against special legislation has been replaced by a general provision prohibiting such laws.

Yet, there still are a number of restrictions in the present constitution. Carried over from the old document are prohibitions against enacting *ex post facto* laws, laws impairing the obligation of a contract, or any special legislation (the new constitution simply provides that the question of what is special legislation shall be judicially determined). New restrictions on the type of legislation the General Assembly can enact are found principally in the local government (VII) and revenue (IX) articles of the new constitution. As discussed earlier, home rule powers granted certain municipalities and counties impose certain limitations on the legislature. Most of these involve a requirement for an extraordinary majority to pass legislation on a particular subject affecting home rule units.

The new revenue article represents one of the real ironies in this area — it is probably more restrictive than the article it replaced in the 1870 constitution. For many years it was believed that the old revenue article prohibited an income tax. One of the major reasons for calling a convention in the late 1960s was this supposed prohibition and the problems inherent under the old article with classifying property, particularly in the large urban counties like Cook, DuPage, Lake, and St. Clair. After the convention call had

20 Ibid., pp. 47, 49.

been approved, the Illinois Supreme Court ruled in *Thorpe* v. *Mahin*[21] that an income tax was constitutional under the old article. The new article, while lacking the old uniformity clause, provides some very tight parameters within which the General Assembly can legislate in both the property and the income tax areas.

The new constitution also imposes several constitutional limitations on how individual legislators can conduct both their public and private lives by requiring that they file according to law a verified statement of their economic interests with the secretary of state. The penalty for failing to file, as set by the constitution, is forfeiture of, or ineligibility for, office. A person convicted of a felony, bribery, perjury, or other heinous crime also becomes ineligible to hold office.

Finally, the legislature cannot delegate its lawmaking power to the people, so there is no general power to pass a statute of statewide impact and submit it to the people for acceptance or rejection as in some other states. Advisory referenda are, of course, a different matter. The legislature may not encroach on the powers of other branches of government, and citizens are protected from its power by the bill of rights. It may not deny equal protection of the laws or due process of law.

REPRESENTATION

Having dealt with the powers of the General Assembly as a collective group, it seems appropriate at this point to consider a very vital role which each one of the 236 legislators performs individually, that is, representing the people of his or her district.

In his essay "Dimensions of State Politics," Herbert Jacob recalls: "Every schoolboy has learned that legislators represent the people. History has known many an autocratic executive, but legislatures have rarely been the engine of oppression. In America, they function as a check on the executive; they are also instrumental in integrating public demands with public policy. . . . The performance of this function is no easy task because the people rarely know what they want and in so far as they do know, they are often divided among themselves."[22]

[21] 43 Ill. 2d 36, 250 N.E.2d 633 (1969).
[22] Herbert Jacob, "Dimensions of State Politics," in *State Legislatures in American Politics*, pp. 5-6.

Constituents — the people back in the district — expect their legislators to act for them, to be their instruments for getting things done. In these terms, Jewell and Patterson tell us, representation may be defined as a kind of activity, a way of acting, or an expectation about how a representative ought to act in place of or in behalf of his constituents.[23]

Among legislators and political philosophers alike there remain clearly divergent views as to how a legislator should act in representing the people of his district. The classic distinction between Hobbes and Burke has filtered down to the present day, with each philosopher continuing to have his own set of contemporary legislators who subscribe to his view.

Thomas Hobbes, seventeenth century English political philosopher and author of the *Leviathan*, held the view that representatives "have authority from them [whom they represent] so far-forth as is in their Commission, but no farther."[24] Hobbes viewed the relationship between the citizen and his representative as strictly a contractual one in which the latter would do precisely as he is instructed to do. Present-day advocates of Hobbes's point of view argue that a legislator should always vote the way his constituents feel. Trying to determine exactly what constituents do believe or feel, however, can often prove to be very difficult.

Edmund Burke, on the other hand, once a member of the English Parliament, held to the "free agent" conception of representation. He supported the notion that a representative ought to be guided by his own best judgment.[25]

An interview study of legislators in four states (California, New Jersey, Ohio, and Tennessee) disclosed that contemporary legislators adopt either of these role orientations or a combination of the two. As identified by the authors of *The Legislative System,* the role orientations are:

"Trustee" — the legislator who sees himself, as Burke did, as a free agent, bound only to follow his conscience and convictions.

[23] Malcolm E. Jewell and Samuel C. Patterson, *The Legislative Process in the United States* (New York: Random House, 1968), pp. 28-40.

[24] Thomas Hobbes, *Leviathan* (London, 1953), p. 84.

[25] Heinz Eulau et al., "The Role of the Representative: Some Empirical Observations on the Theory of Edmund Burke," *American Political Science Review* 53 (1959):742-56.

"Delegate" — the legislator who senses a strong obligation to consult constituents and to follow their instructions, essentially the Hobbesian role.

"Politico" — the legislator who holds both trustee and delegate role orientations, alternating between them.[26]

Regardless of how they view their role, most legislators do endeavor to represent their constituents in two ways: by initiating and supporting legislation that confers advantages in their districts and by performing personal services or running errands for constituents. How much time a legislator devotes to these functions is probably dependent on his perception of his role and the margin by which he won election. There are probably many Illinois legislators who spend a majority of their time handling the "casework" of their constituents, although this situation is gradually changing as legislators have started to receive more staff help and clerical assistance.

REAPPORTIONMENT

Apportionment and the drawing of legislative district lines are important techniques of representation which have become especially controversial in recent years. No method of representation extends equally to all individuals, and none is politically neutral. "The process of apportionment," according to Alfred de Grazia, "is a point of entry for preferred social values. The existing system of apportionment, whether legal, illegal, or extra-legal, institutionalizes the values of some group in a society."[27]

Section 3 of the legislative article of the 1970 Illinois Constitution requires that the General Assembly redistrict the fifty-nine legislative districts in the year following each federal decennial census year. The districts are to be "compact, contiguous and substantially equal in population." The redistricting plan must be approved and effective by June 30 of that year, or, as happened in 1971, a legislative

[26] John C. Wahlke et al., *The Legislative System: Explorations in Legislative Behavior* (New York: John Wiley, 1962), p. 281. This study found that a solid majority of the legislators in each of the four states held the trustee or free-agent orientation toward their role as representatives of the people. About a quarter of the legislators interviewed classified themselves as politicos, while only about one-seventh viewed themselves as delegates.

[27] Alfred de Grazia, "General Theory of Apportionment," *Law and Contemporary Problems* 17 (1952):257.

redistricting commission must be formed within ten days. With co-terminous districts, both Senate and House members are vitally concerned with how the lines are redrawn. Coupled with stringent requirements for population equality, redistricting means that one change made in a proposed map may ripple across the entire map, affecting literally dozens of incumbents in both houses. With the Republicans holding a narrow edge in the House, and neither party alone able to pass a bill in the Senate, it was not totally surprising then that as July 1, 1971, dawned the legislature was still without a new apportionment plan.

In situations such as this, the new constitution provides that the speaker and minority leader of the House and the president and minority leader of the Senate each shall appoint one member from among his own legislative ranks and one member from outside the General Assembly. These eight members then have thirty days in which to organize and file a redistricting plan. A simple majority, or five members, is required for a plan to be approved.

The failure of five members of the commission to agree on a plan by the end of this period results in the random choice of a tie breaker (one of two persons of different political parties named by the supreme court and drawn by the secretary of state). Thus, one political party or the other should gain a majority on the commission by luck of the draw. This step was not utilized in 1971 as the commission succeeded in filing a plan approved by a vote of 6 to 2 with the secretary of state prior to the August 10 deadline.[28]

Every even-numbered year at the general election in November, between 19 and 39 of the Senate's 59 members and all of the House's 177 members are up for election. In 1972 two-thirds of the senators up for election were running for four-year terms, the other third for two-year terms. This third had to stand for election

[28] Subsequently the Illinois Supreme Court invalidated this plan on the ground that the commission was illegally constituted. The court ruled that three of the legislative leaders violated the intent of Art. IV, sec. 3(b), when they each appointed a member of their staff to serve as their non-General Assembly member on the commission. The court also held that the same three leaders improperly appointed themselves to the commission. The commission's work product was approved by the court as a provisional redistricting plan for the election of members of the General Assembly in 1972. An amended opinion mandated the 1973-74 General Assembly to adopt a permanent plan in 1973, which it did by reenacting the same map. See *People* ex rel. *Scott* v. *Grivetti,* 50 Ill. 2d 156, 277 N.E.2d 881 (1971).

again in 1974, only this time for four-year terms. The other two-thirds of the senators ran in 1976, half for four-year terms and the other half for two-year terms. Thus, during the decade in which each redistricting plan is supposed to be applicable, each seat comes up for election three times, twice for four-year terms, once for a two-year term.

Under a system of cumulative voting unique to Illinois, three members of the House of Representatives are elected from each of the state's fifty-nine legislative districts for two-year terms. Designed to give the minority party in each district one of the three seats, cumulative voting allows a voter to cast three votes for one candidate or to distribute his or her votes among two or three candidates. By "plumping" three votes for one of its candidates, the minority party can ordinarily insure the election of at least one member of its party from that district. The new constitution prohibits a political party from limiting its nominations to fewer than two candidates in each district. Since 1930 the minority party has only once held less than 42 percent of the seats.[29] In contrast, minority representation in the Senate has dropped as low as 25 percent.

While the partisan division in the House has been extremely close over the years, the Republican party has clearly had the edge. Since 1920, the Democrats have had a majority in only six biennia. During this same period the Republicans have also dominated the Senate. Before 1971-72, when a 29-29 split occurred, the Democrats had been in control for only four sessions (1933-39) during the preceding half century. The period of Republican dominance may be at an end, however, as the Democrats have made inroads into traditionally Republican downstate districts. In 1974, the Democrats won control of both houses.

[29] After an unprecedented at-large election in 1964, the Republicans occupied only one-third of the seats in the House. See Charles W. Dunn, "Cumulative Voting Problems in Illinois Legislative Elections," *Harvard Journal on Legislation* 9 (1972):627-65.

2

The Legislature in Operation

To accomplish its primary task of lawmaking, the General Assembly has established certain procedures, some in accordance with constitutional requirements, but most by rule, to provide for orderly operation with safeguards against unwise and hasty actions. Because the Illinois legislature is a bicameral body, certain operational procedures facilitate movement of legislative business between the houses. The procedures and practices vary at different periods of the session with the workload of pending legislation.

As a result of one of the many changes brought about by the new Illinois Constitution, the General Assembly is now required to convene *each* year on the second Wednesday of January. The 1870 state constitution did not set a terminal date for each legislative session (nor does the 1970 constitution), specifying only that the legislature convene on the Wednesday after the first Monday in January of each odd-numbered year. The custom had been for both houses to adjourn *sine die* (without setting a date to return) by June 30 and not convene again until the next regularly scheduled session eighteen months later. The six-month length of each biennial session had become an established pattern largely in response to the (old) constitutional provision that "no act of the General Assembly shall take effect until the first day of July next after its passage, unless in case of emergency, the General Assembly shall, by a vote of two-thirds of all members elected to each house, otherwise direct." Thus, the legislature was not required to adjourn by midnight on June 30 but it always found this to be at least a psychological limitation on the length of a session because any measure passed with less than a two-thirds majority would not take effect until the following July 1.[1]

Although annual sessions are now required by the constitution, they were already being used through the device of recessed sessions prior to the adoption of the new charter. Largely in response to a recommendation from the Commission on the Organization of the General Assembly, which had been established in 1965 to consider ways of improving the legislative branch, the 1967 General Assembly became the first assembly since 1907-08 not to adjourn *sine die* on June 30 of the odd-numbered year. Instead, it returned for "recessed sessions" in the fall of 1967 and the following spring to consider gubernatorial vetoes, organize interim commissions, and consider several administration requests. This practice was carried on into the next General Assembly except that by the spring of 1970 the legislature was meeting for two months instead of several days as it deliberated over the governor's second annual budget.

The spring session of 1972 was the first even-year session formally mandated by the constitution, but an attempt was again made to limit consideration to appropriation and revenue matters. Although the attempt was not completely successful, the session was sufficiently restricted in scope to be called a budgetary session. Senate Rule 5 specifically limited these sessions by barring introduction of any nonbudgetary bills except those approved by the Rules Committee. This has since been changed to permit the introduction of any bill in an even-numbered year, but to require that all bills except those that implement the state budget or are introduced by standing committees be automatically referred to the Rules Committee in either house. It then takes a majority vote of the Rules Committee to assign any bill to a substantive committee. Only the affirmative vote of a majority of those elected to either house can reverse the decision of the Rules Committee not to release a bill for committee consideration. While each biennium the legislature has found itself meeting for a longer period of time during the even

[1] As discussed briefly at the end of Chapter 1, the division between the two major parties in the House has always been very close. Hence, unless both sides of the aisle had agreed to a particular proposal, it was impossible to muster the extraordinary majority needed to pass "emergency" bills.

year, and considering more and more nonbudgetary legislation, the major business and purpose of the spring sessions remains the adoption of a state budget.

Annual sessions continue to have many vocal and respected critics who fear that Illinois is inching ever closer to a full-time legislature which will ultimately force into retirement many good people who have served as citizen-legislators. Others suggest that the state is spending more money because of annual sessions and annual appropriations. For these reasons several prominent elected officials have urged the adoption of a constitutional amendment limiting the even-year sessions solely to money matters and limiting them to ninety days. Thus far such moves have failed, although the General Assembly has attempted to achieve the same end through its legislative rules.

Social and economic conditions are placing ever growing demands on state government which are beyond either the governor's or the legislature's control. The workload of the General Assembly cannot help but increase with each coming year. Only the proper phasing of deadlines at various stages in the legislative process and the increased use of a working committee system can prevent the legislature from being in session more and more days each year. Even that may not help. Whatever the solution or outcome, it is unreasonable to expect the state's problems to go away simply because the legislature is not in session.

Recent Fall Sessions

Because it is now a continuous body and standing committees remain alive for the entire biennium, the General Assembly no longer has to adhere to the practice of recessing until immediately before a new General Assembly convenes. Fall sessions have continued to be utilized each year so that the General Assembly can consider emergency matters and executive vetoes. They also allow the Senate to act more expeditiously on gubernatorial appointments.

Fall sessions have also lessened the chance that a bill will be caught in the usual end-of-the-session "logjam" and not be considered before June 30. With bills carrying over from one session to another during a given biennium, action is more easily delayed on bills (of both major and minor importance) which a reluctant majority might have passed in prior years. Sponsors have helped to reduce the crush of the logjam (a problem common to all legislatures) by not pressing their bills at the end of June. Controversial bills and bills of limited effect are now frequently carried over for study by a joint subcommittee or legislative commission during the interim between spring and fall sessions.

Special Sessions

The governor, and the presiding officers of both houses acting jointly, have the constitutional power to convene special sessions by proclamation. The governor may also convene the Senate alone. The governor's proclamation must state the explicit purpose for convening the legislature, and, except for impeachments or confirmation of appointments, no other matters may be considered. The governor's judgment that a special session is called for is final and not subject to review by the courts.[2] Under the old constitution this device was used only infrequently, partly because of the difficulty of mustering the two-thirds vote that was necessary for legislation to be effective prior to the following July 1. The new constitution relaxes that requirement only slightly to a three-fifths majority. One outcome of the special session may be to serve the governor as an instrument to remedy legislative oversight. Special sessions have also been used as a means of restricting the agenda of a fall veto session, and in the fall of 1973 there were five concurrent special sessions meeting largely because of this reason.

Under the new constitution the presiding officers of both houses are also able to convene special sessions by means of a joint proclamation. The legislature has provided by law that the limitations on special sessions called by the governor apply to special sessions called by the General Assembly. The first such special session was convened in October 1973, one of the five concurrent sessions mentioned above.

---

[2] *Herzberger* v. *Kelly*, 366 Ill. 126, 7 N.E.2d 865 (1937). The fact that a special session is being held does not prevent the governor from calling other special sessions to run concurrently. See also *People* ex rel. *Kell* v. *Kramer*, 328 Ill. 512, 160 N.E. 60 (1928).

PROROGUE

The governor has the additional constitutional power to prorogue (adjourn) the General Assembly if a disagreement arises between the two houses over the time of adjournment. If such a disagreement does exist, formal notice by either house must be sent to the governor before he can officially proclaim the legislature adjourned. The governor last invoked this power in November 1970, when the House, having already adjourned to a later date, would not accede to the request made by the Senate that both houses adjourn *sine die*.

PERFUNCTORY SESSIONS

Both the House and Senate once made generous use of perfunctory sessions to speed up the mechanics of the legislative process. In recent years this practice has been almost eliminated as the existence of the verbatim transcripts raises the question of whether bills read during a perfunctory session, when a quorum is obviously not present, meet the constitutional requirement of three readings.

A perfunctory session, when it is held, is attended by only a handful of legislators; by informal agreement only routine business is transacted. A quorum is not present and nothing is brought up that would occasion a roll call. The perfunctory session is used to expedite bill introductions, advancements to second reading, committee reports, and other kinds of legislative activity that, for one reason or another, are necessary but automatic and time-consuming. Perfunctory sessions in both houses, when they occur, usually come at the end of the legislative workweek when most legislators have gone home for the weekend.

DEADLINES

The logjams discussed above also have been diminished somewhat by the adoption of joint House and Senate rules prescribing a timetable for the introduction and final passage of all bills except annual appropriations for state agencies, committee bills, and bills deemed by a majority of the Rules Committee of either house to be emergency bills necessary for the operation of government. Bills may usually be introduced no later than sixty days before June 30. The timetables also set final dates for committee and floor action first in the house of origin, then in the second house. In 1973 the House moved a step further and adopted rules which impose running deadlines with respect to each bill. For instance, a bill must be reported out of committee within forty-five days of assignment to that committee or it is automatically tabled. (For some time the Senate has had a similar sixty-day rule, but it is rarely invoked.) Appropriation bills are excepted from this rule. The only way around this time limit is by a vote of two-thirds of the committee members to place a bill on the committee's interim study calendar. This allows the committee to hold hearings and take testimony, but no bills placed on the interim study calendar can be reported to the floor before the beginning of the second year of the biennium except by a three-fifths vote of all the members elected to the House. Once on the calendar, a bill must pass the House in thirty days or it is automatically tabled. The House imposes an additional requirement with respect to its own bills which directs that such bills pass the chamber on or before May 25 of the year in which they are introduced regardless of how many of the thirty days remain.

As more and more legislation is considered in each session, it is easy to imagine how the entire legislative process could come to a complete and chaotic halt without these rules. Even with the deadlines there are two or three smaller, but more manageable, logjams as bill introductions are finally cut off, and as the last day for passage of bills in the house of origin, and later the second house, is reached. Certain bills, like budgetary bills, are excepted, but by and large the deadlines serve as identifiable focal points in each session. In 1975 each of the deadlines set forth in the joint rules was met without any suspensions or day-to-day extensions. As a result the General Assembly missed its target recess date of June 30 by only two days.

Table 1 shows the total number of bills introduced by months for the last six regular sessions, plus the introductions in fall and even-year spring sessions. For the 1975-76 General Assembly only bills introduced during 1975 are included. Both Senate and House bills are grouped together; with the exception of the 1971-72 biennium, when the Senate accounted for only about a fourth of the

TABLE 1. BILL INTRODUCTIONS, 1965-75

	Number of Bills					
	1965	1967	1969	1971	1973	1975
Spring of odd year						
January	386	678	323	342	289	316
February	558	402	756	549	419	437
March	894	1,020	1,004	1,238	669	975
April	493	1,415	2,008	1,966	1,678	2,760
May	928	706	93	40	109	38
June	331	47	15	672	42	107
July	*	*	*	*	4	2
	3,590	4,268	4,199	4,807	3,210	4,635
Fall of odd year	*	30	77	277	282	132
Spring of even year	*	580	1,122	1,217	1,216	NA
Summer of even year	*	193	*	*	*	NA
Fall of even year	*	*	0	42	16	NA
Totals	3,590	5,071	5,398	6,343	4,724	4,767

* Legislature did not meet.

total, the ratio has generally been about one Senate bill to every two House bills.

In 1965, the last session before these deadlines were adopted, there were 1,259 bills introduced in May and June. In 1967, with the imposition of a May 1 cut-off date for bill introductions, there were only 66 bills filed after that date (687 were introduced on May 1). Except in 1971 when there was a breakdown of this rule in the House, every succeeding session has been in sharp contrast to the 1965 session. The deadlines have been pushed back over the intervening years so that the deadline is now usually sometime in mid-April.

The deadline for reporting bills out of committee also has an impact on the tempo of the first few months of the session — both houses generally meet only two or three days a week through the month of March. It is during this period and on into April and early May that committee hearings consume the major portion of the time spent by the legislators in Springfield. The new House rules seem complex and have taken some getting used to by veteran members, but they have served their purpose in pushing bills along earlier in the session. The forty-five-day committee rule has meant that some bills which were introduced early in the session must be reported to the floor by early March or be tabled.[3] This appears to have helped spread out House committee workloads, many of which have recently been subject to the same kinds of logjams experienced on the floor.

In recent years the period from January through April has also been characterized by the submission of reports by interim study commissions. An intensive review of the governor's budget is made after he presents it on March 1 and prior to formal committee hearings. During this period, when major fiscal policy decisions have yet to be made and with commission or committee studies incomplete, the legislature is loathe to take conclusive action on any legislation of major import. Emphasis in each house centers on getting that house's own bills out of committee, and this is followed by a period of several weeks in May when each body then seeks to amend (if necessary) and pass its own bills. Each house has required by rule that all bills originating in that chamber be passed before the end of the fourth week in May. As these bills begin to move out of committee, and as the deadline for introduction of bills passes, the tempo of legislative activity naturally picks up. In recent years the General Assembly has spent almost as many days in session during the month of May as it has in June.

END OF THE SESSION

As each house clears its calendar of the bills which originated in that body, the days and weeks begin to get longer with committees now considering bills received from the second house, looking toward the reporting deadline in mid-June. Because the intensity of activity on the floor of each house never seems to wane at this point, committees may have to meet early in the day or late at night in order to complete their work (since they are not ordinarily permitted to meet when the parent body is in session).

The result of all this has been that in recent years both houses have usually been in full session at least twenty days during May, and in June for as many as twenty-five out of the thirty days, gen-

[3] During the first session this rule was in effect, 224 bills were tabled as a result of it; only three of these bills were successfully revived later. One of the major advantages of this change has been that it prevents the springing of bad bills at the end of the session.

erally meeting straight through the weekend during the last ten days. Prior to the adoption of the series of deadlines, unmanageably heavy workloads characterized the closing days of the session, and the daily calendars, listing the bills eligible for consideration each day on a single large sheet of paper, approached the size of the proverbial bedsheet.[4]

Stopping the Clock

Although the pace at the end of June has been considerably less chaotic in the past several sessions, the General Assembly has still been forced to utilize the time-honored device of "stopping the clock." The practice has developed because of the effective date given legislation passed after June 30. To create the appearance of final legislative action before July 1, the clocks located at the rear of the House and Senate chambers are often stopped shortly before midnight. Legislative action might take place after midnight according to the observer's watch, but the official entry in the House and Senate journals will show that passage took place prior to adjournment. The time of adjournment is designated on the stopped clock. The courts have directly validated this practice by refusing to recognize evidence other than what is officially recorded in the journals of the General Assembly.[5] Thus the legislature has often

[4] House Rule 37(c) (thirty-day rule) apparently was somewhat successful in pushing advancement of bills on the calendar: only eleven bills were tabled as a result of this rule in 1973 and eighteen in 1974. Five of the bills tabled in 1974 were Senate bills which ultimately reached the governor after being taken from the table and passed. The use of calendars is discussed in detail in Chapter 3.

[5] *Sangamon County Fair and Agricultural Association* v. *Stanard,* 9 Ill. 2d 267, 137 N.E.2d 487 (1956). This decision was rendered during the life of the old constitution. However, in an unpublished opinion to the governor on House Bill 1954, dated September 6, 1972, Attorney General William J. Scott noted "that it was the intent of the framers [of the 1970 constitution] to adopt the enrolled bill rule. This rule provides that once the proper officers place their signatures upon a bill it must be conclusively presumed that all constitutionally required procedures have been followed in the enactment of the bill." Scott said this meant the courts are prevented from going behind the face of the bill and looking at journal entries, copies of the original bill, amendments thereto, or hearing testimony pertaining to the legislative history of the bill. This change from the "journal entry rule" validated by the *Sangamon County Fair* case to the "enrolled bill rule" was apparently designed, Scott said, to eliminate unnecessary litigation generated by the former rule. Scott's conclusion was that basically the "enrolled bill rule" is a limitation only upon judicial review, and that the extent of this limitation must be precisely defined by the Illinois courts.

been able to squeeze a few more useful hours of life from each June 30. Even these last extra hours have not always been enough for the legislature to complete its business. As a result, both houses have in recent years acknowledged that they have passed the magic line into July, sometimes for days. This, of course, changes the number of votes required for passage of legislation from a simple majority to a three-fifths majority, thereby strengthening the last-minute bargaining position of the minority party.

SOURCES OF ORGANIZATION AND PROCEDURE

Knowledge of the legislative provisions of the 1970 Illinois Constitution is fundamental to an understanding of the machinery of the legislative process. The legislative article (IV) of the constitution has an enormous impact on the character of the legislative process and the subsequent strategies involved in the passage of bills. It provides when the General Assembly shall convene, limits the effective date of legislation, requires three readings of the title of each bill and a roll call vote on final passage, limits bills — except those for appropriations and for the codification, revision, or rearrangement of laws — to one subject, allows bills to originate in either house, requires a majority of all members elected for final approval of legislation, provides a number of means by which the governor can approve or veto legislation, and determines how members are elected.

Rules Adopted by Each House

The constitution also permits each house to "determine the rules of its proceedings, judge the elections, returns and qualifications of its members and choose its officers." The rules adopted by each house fill in the skeletal framework erected by the constitution. House and Senate rules, while not necessarily uniform, are primarily applicable to floor procedure, committee structure, amendments, decorum, and other procedural aspects of the legislative process. The formal rules create an orderly routine as bills travel the customary path of committee referral, three readings, and roll call votes on final passage. Occasionally, efforts may be made to disrupt the routine by legislators interested in the passage or defeat of a particular bill. Members may attempt to nonconcur in a committee recommendation, discharge a committee, or compose formal disagreements between the houses. On any procedure established by rule, however, a majority of the members elected will prevail, unless the rules specifically provide otherwise.[6]

Not all regulations affecting the legislator and his problems can be found in either the rules of the two houses or, when adopted by both houses, in the joint rules which govern relations between the two chambers. Sometimes there is a wide gap between the range of procedures laid out by rule and actual legislative behavior. Situations not covered by the rules are likely to be governed by *Robert's Rules of Order Newly Revised*. In fact, the rules of each house specifically state that *Robert's Rules of Order Newly Revised* applies in those situations not governed by the formal rules. Just as significant are the informal rules that have become customary guides to legislative conduct.

House and Senate Journals

The constitution also directs that each house keep and publish a journal of its proceedings. Although the constitution requires that only the record vote on passage (or a record vote requested by two members of the Senate or five members of the House) be entered in the journal, each step necessary to final passage is recorded. The journals record each bill as it is introduced and read by title on

---

[6] This was true in the Senate during both the 1973-74 General Assembly and the 1975-76 General Assembly, where thirty votes could do anything, including the all-important suspension of the rules. The only exception was a motion to overrule a ruling of the chair, which required a three-fifths majority. In the 1971-72 General Assembly a three-fifths majority had been required to suspend the rules.

In the House a three-fifths majority (107 votes) has been required in a significant number of situations. Since 1973 the extraordinary majority has been required to discharge a bill from an interim study calendar, advance a bill to second reading without reference, or suspend any one of eleven rules having to do with posting of committee hearing notices, deadline for introduction of bills, tabling of bills reported out of committee "do not pass," deadline on final passage of House bills, the thirty-day limit on calling of bills on the calendar, assignment of resolutions including those proposing constitutional amendments, reconsideration of any votes, motions to take from the table, conference committee reports, and, of course, the amendment or suspension of the rules.

three separate legislative days. All amendments offered on second reading are printed in full, as are resolutions, committee reports, and messages from the governor and the other house. The journals are prepared by the clerk of the House and the secretary of the Senate after each day's business, sent to the printer, and distributed to the membership on the next legislative day. (Toward the end of the session there is often a lag of several days before printed journals are received.) Reports from standing committees state only the recommended committee action, and neither the committee reports nor the journals contain any statements on or explanation of legislation as discussed in committee or debated on the floor.

Although the 1870 constitution contained a provision that allowed for the inclusion in the journals of protests on the part of members or others who felt that the majority action as recorded was not legal or was not fair to the minority, this is now simply part of the rules of both houses. Nevertheless, any two members of either house still have the right to have their protest printed, in respectful language, in the journal. Similarly, two members of the Senate or five of the House are permitted to demand that the yeas and nays be recorded on any question. Roll call votes are frequently taken at legislative steps earlier than the final passage of bills, particularly on controversial matters, and the journals show the names of members voting for and against a question. In fact, a large part of the space on journal pages is taken up with roll calls.

In the end, however, the journals of both houses provide only a sketchy outline of the actions of the General Assembly. They are of little value in determining legislative intent and provide only the basic evidence that constitutional provisions regarding the enactment of bills have been followed.[7]

---

[7] Under the old constitution it was possible for a bill, even if it had been authenticated by the signatures of the presiding officers of both houses and signed by the governor, to be invalidated if an examination of the journals showed noncompliance with constitutionally prescribed procedures. The Illinois Supreme Court is apparently not going to permit such challenges under the "enrolled bill rule" of the new constitution. In a 1974 decision, the court stated: "Whether or not a bill has been read by title, as the Constitution commands, seems fairly to be characterized as a procedural matter, the determination of which was deliberately left to the presiding officers of the two houses of the General Assembly." See *Fuehrmeyer* v. *City of Chicago* and *City of Evanston* v. *Department of Registration and Education,* 57 Ill. 2d 193, 311 N.E.2d 116 (1974). See also footnote 5 above.

Transcript of Debates

Besides carrying over from the 1870 constitution the requirement that each house keep and publish a journal, the 1970 constitution imposes a new requirement that each house keep a transcript of its debates and that the transcript be made available for public inspection.[8]

Since this requirement took effect July 1, 1971, both houses have been recording and transcribing their debates. The transcripts are then filed by the secretary of the Senate and the clerk of the House with the secretary of state, who is charged under the provisions of a 1974 law with maintaining them as a public record and making them available for public inspection. The cost of reproducing these transcripts must be borne by the person or institution making the request. This procedure is still relatively new, but already it has resulted in a number of court decisions which refer directly to the transcripts. Courts are now able to review these transcripts for the purpose of determining "legislative intent." All the ramifications of this provision have yet to be felt, but some are already proving to be significant.

Quorum Requirements

Attendance requirements are intended as safeguards against action without adequate representation. The quorum (or minimum number of members of each house of the General Assembly that may transact the business of that house) is set by the constitution at a majority — more than half — of the total elected membership. This

[8] The governor's veto message on House Bill 1954, 1971-72 General Assembly (House *Journal*, vol. 2, pp. 10970-74 (1972)), states: "The transcript should cover any stage of a bill when legislative debate and discussion would throw light on the legislative intent. ... Section 7(b) of Article IV of the Illinois Constitution of 1970 does not require a transcript of debates and proceedings in committees of the General Assembly. ... The [1969-70 Illinois Constitutional Convention] debates made clear that there was no intention by the convention to require publication of the transcript of debates as distinguished from the journal; also, that it would be sufficient if a single copy of the transcript were prepared and kept in the office of an appropriate official of each House and made available for public examination. ... It was the intention that any person desiring a copy would be able to secure the same at his own expense."

See also the opinion of Attorney General William J. Scott to the Honorable W. Robert Blair, File No. S-461, May 30, 1972.

means eighty-nine members in the House and thirty in the Senate. In the House, the speaker orders the roll taken to ascertain attendance. In the Senate, the presiding officer may proceed with business if he considers a quorum present, but if a senator questions the presence of a quorum, the roll is called.

In either house, the number of members present on the floor during a session may be less than a quorum. Should it develop as the result of a roll call in either house that a quorum is not present, the names of the absentees are called again. If a quorum fails, those present may adjourn or, by majority vote, may compel the attendance of the absentees by sending out officers to take them in custody and bring them before the body.

Statutes

The *Illinois Revised Statutes* (particularly Chapter 63 dealing with the General Assembly and Chapter 127 dealing with state government generally) also define some aspects of legislative functioning even though they have little direct impact on legislative procedure and organization. In regard to the latter, however, the statutes do provide for the prefiling of bills in the month preceding the convening of each new General Assembly, outline the hearing procedure before legislative committees and commissions, require filing of fiscal and judicial notes with certain types of bills, define the police power of the General Assembly, and provide for a uniform effective date of laws. Requirements pertaining to the filing of economic disclosure forms and disclosure of campaign spending practices are also covered.

There are five major permanent agencies supporting the legislature — the Legislative Council, the Legislative Reference Bureau, the Illinois Intergovernmental Cooperation Commission, the Economic and Fiscal Commission, and the Legislative Audit Commission — created by statute, as well as other auxiliary groups such as the Legislative Space Needs Commission, the Legislative Investigating Commission, and the Commission to Visit and Examine State Institutions. A number of permanent, as well as interim, research commissions which study ongoing or topical problems between regular sessions are also created by statute.

The House of Representatives and the Senate both elect their own presiding officers. The constitution provides that the secretary of state shall convene the House on the first day of the January session in the odd-numbered year for the purpose of electing a speaker from its membership to serve as presiding officer. Similarly, the governor is to convene the Senate for the purpose of electing a president from among its membership. In the House the speaker appoints a majority leader, who serves as his floor leader and first lieutenant. In the Senate the president is both the presiding officer and the majority leader. The minority leader in each chamber is a member of the numerically strongest political party other than the party to which the speaker (in the House) or president (in the Senate) belongs. All four leaders then traditionally choose several assistant leaders to serve as their whips during the next two years.

Once it elects its leaders for the coming session, each house organizes separately for its own operation. Each has its own officers, employees, and committee structure.

RELATIONS BETWEEN THE TWO CHAMBERS

At every session of the legislature there are occasional joint sessions of the two houses sitting as a single assembly. These are primarily ceremonial meetings; laws are never passed then.

Immediately after the houses have elected their officers, the General Assembly meets in a joint session to hear the governor report on the condition of the state and recommend such measures as he deems desirable. It is also customary for the two houses to meet again in joint session to hear the governor present his budget. Thereafter, similar joint sessions may be held to hear any further message the governor wishes to deliver in person, or to hear patriotic, memorial, or other addresses on special occasions such as Lincoln's birthday, or when members of both houses wish to hear a distinguished guest, such as a foreign dignitary. Although the governor's messages need not be delivered in person, the governor usually does appear before a joint session of the two houses for such occasions. Such an appearance, in person, assures the fullest possible attention for his message since it will be reported not only in the printed media but also on television and radio. Almost all joint sessions are held in the chambers of the House of Representatives.

On all other occasions and for all other formal business, the General Assembly acts as two separate bodies and effects common action only through the exchange of official messages between the houses on the basis of formal action of each house separately; or, in the case of disagreement after the exchange of messages on the final text of bills passed by both houses, by establishing conference committees composed of selected members from the two houses. Of course, members of the two houses can, as individuals or as influential political party leaders, facilitate common action, and they may appear, and do so as bill sponsors, as witnesses before the committees of the other house. Such individual methods of influence toward comman action between the houses are informal and are not clothed with authority.

Each of these sources of legislative procedure and organization contributes to a set of rules — "the rules of the game" — that dictate the ebb and flow of legislative behavior. A thorough knowledge of formal rule and custom is necessary for success in moving a bill over the obstacles strewn on the path to final passage.

3

Lawmaking

The legislature gives formal expression to its actions by means of bills, resolutions, and motions. If acted upon favorably, bills are "passed"; resolutions and motions are "adopted." Bills when passed and signed by the governor become "acts," "enactments," "laws," or "statutes" — in a general way all four terms mean about the same thing. Bills and joint resolutions must be passed in identical form and wording by both houses of the General Assembly.

THE NATURE OF BILLS

Bills are proposed changes in or additions to the existing body of statute law and comprise the major legislative product both in quantity and in impact.[1] A bill is identified by its number, its author or sponsor, and its title. Bills may be introduced into the General Assembly only by members (or by committees) and are known as Senate or House bills depending on the chamber where introduced. For brevity and ease of identification, bills are listed as, for example, S.B. 55 or H.B. 112, bearing the number corresponding to the order of their introduction in their respective houses.

Constitutional Requirements

The constitution requires that the final vote of "yeas and nays" on passage in each house be recorded in the journal of that house. The

---

[1] Appropriation bills are only temporary additions and as such are not printed in the *Illinois Revised Statutes*.

number of votes in favor of passage on that final action in each
house must be equal to at least a majority of the entire elected membership of that house. Referred to as a "constitutional majority,"
this constitutes at least thirty affirmative votes in the Senate and
eighty-nine in the House.[2]

The constitution of 1970 still provides for the traditional three
readings except that, instead of requiring that each bill "be read at
large," it merely requires that a "bill shall be read by title on three
different days in each house." This conforms with the procedure
the General Assembly has usually followed in the past. The time
requirements and the fact that the legislature found it necessary to
provide for a number of other steps in the procedure contributed
significantly to this development. Thus, the traditional three readings
of a bill have been just three steps or stages in a much longer list
of procedural actions that transform a bill into law. Moreover, the
printing of bills and adopted amendments has served as a basis for
common reference before any serious consideration of a bill takes
place, and has proved to be both far more accurate and far less
time consuming than oral reading.

Bills introduced in the General Assembly generally fall into two
categories — those which amend existing statutes and those which
are new law. As was pointed out in the first chapter, the constitution
requires that each bill must contain an enacting clause to indicate the origin of legislative authority. Thus a joint resolution cannot
have the force of law since it does not have an enacting clause.[3]

Two other constitutional provisions also affect the form of bills.
Each bill, except those for appropriations and for the codification,
revision, or rearrangement of laws, is limited to one subject.[4] Appro-

---

[2] Final action is the last constitutionally required action of the General
Assembly before a bill becomes law. Final action may be passage in the house
of origin when the second house passes the bill without amendment; it may be
the vote in concurring on amendments made in the second house; it may be
the vote accepting a conference report; it may be the vote accepting or rejecting the governor's specific recommendations for change; or it may be the vote
overriding the governor's veto.

[3] *Burritt* v. *Commissioners of State Contracts,* 120 Ill. 322, 11 N.E. 180
(1887) and *Wenner* v. *Thornton,* 98 Ill. 156 (1880). The attorney general ruled
in 1910 that a bill was unconstitutional if it contained an enacting clause that
varied at all from the form specified in the constitution. See *Report of the
Attorney General,* 1910, p. 77.

[4] The old constitutional requirement that the subject of each bill must be
expressed in the title was not retained in the 1970 constitution. The constitu-

priation bills are further limited solely to appropriations. In the past, even with the single-subject limitation, an appropriation to the agency was often included in a bill spelling out new duties for that agency because the appropriation would be an essential part of the subject.

The constitution also requires that a "bill expressly amending a law shall set forth completely the sections amended." This new provision should have the effect of clarifying the "principles" developed in the "amendment by reference" cases under the 1870 constitution. In these cases the Illinois Supreme Court interpreted the old constitutional provision to apply to legislation that is amendatory in effect as well as form.[5] The prohibition against amendment by reference has two consequences for the bill-drafting process. First, it requires that in preparing legislation that amends an existing statute the amended section of the law be set out in full within the body of the amendatory bill. Second, other sections of the existing law which are being amended by reference must also be set out in full. This can now generally be done as separate sections or divisions of the same bill as long as they all relate to the same general title. Under the old constitution, a separate bill was required for each act that was amended. Each session a number of nonsubstantive revisions must be made to combine multiple versions of various sections of the statutes which result from the passage of more than one bill amending the same section during the previous session. In 1971 (the last session before the effective date of the new constitution) 341 companion bills were required to accomplish this purpose, while

tional convention's Legislative Committee recommended the elimination of this requirement because "the complexity of many bills considered today defies a thorough expression in title." See *Rouse* v. *Thompson,* 228 Ill. 522, 81 N.E. 1109 (1907). This particular change accounts for the dramatic drop in bill introductions in the 1973-74 General Assembly as compared to the 1971-72 General Assembly (see Table 1) as the large number of companion bills is no longer required.

[5] See, e.g., *People* ex rel. *Gant* v. *Crossley,* 261 Ill. 78, 98, 103 N.E. 537, 540 (1913). In setting boundaries for the application of this constitutional provision to bills that are not expressly amendatory in form, the Illinois Supreme Court has laid down two general criteria: (1) a new act is not invalid as an amendment by reference if it is clearly complete in itself, even though it may affect other acts, and (2) an act is incomplete and invalid as an amendment by reference if it is necessary to read the new act together with an existing act to determine the law.

in 1973 only 2 were required. This change in the use of companion bills has resulted in significantly fewer bill introductions.

Appropriation Bills

Appropriation bills could easily constitute an additional category of legislation. A major portion of each legislative session (particularly in even-numbered years) is devoted to the appropriation of funds for the "ordinary and contingent expenses" of state government.

Procedure on appropriation bills deviates but slightly from that on other bills. There is no constitutional difference in the powers of the two houses on appropriations. The timing in the introduction and passage of fiscal measures may, however, affect the timing and processing of other legislation.

The objects and purposes of appropriations are classified and standardized by statute law, and these categories normally are followed in drafting appropriation bills. There is nothing, however, to prevent deviations in specific appropriation measures. The so-called "major objects" for appropriation purposes are spelled out and defined in the State Finance Act. These objects include personal services, contractual services, travel, commodities, equipment, permanent improvements, land, electronic data processing, operation of automotive equipment, telecommunications, and contingencies.

By passing an appropriations bill, the General Assembly is simply authorizing an agency of state government to expend a certain amount of money. That agency may spend less than the authorization (and indeed, if the agency is directly under the governor, his Bureau of the Budget may force it to), but it may not spend more.[6] An attempt has been made in recent years to combine the appro-

[6] This discussion of an appropriation as an authorization to expend funds from the state treasury should not be confused with the appropriations procedure in Congress. Expenditures by the federal government normally involve a two-step process. First, a substantive legislative committee must authorize a program or activity and authorize the expenditure of money to finance it. Secondly, the Appropriations Committee must give some agency the authority to spend the money to carry out the program which has been authorized. This procedure involves two separate pieces of legislation — an authorization bill and an appropriation bill. The Appropriations Committee's job is to grant authority to someone to spend money for a program already created by an act

priations for several related agencies into one bill, thereby reducing the total number of appropriation bills. This practice has, however, met with mixed results.

Emergency Bills

Passed between July 1 and December 31 of any year, these bills must contain a clause providing for a specific effective date if they are to take effect prior to the normal date of the next July 1. Emergency legislation usually takes effect as soon as it is signed by the governor although this depends on the specific provision in the bill. An emergency act requires an extraordinary majority of three-fifths of the full membership of each house, or 36 yea votes in the Senate and 107 in the House of Representatives. If such a bill receives a majority, but fails to receive the required three-fifths vote, it is automatically reconsidered with the effective date clause removed. Thus, on the subsequent roll call a simple majority will be all that is required for passage.

BILL PREPARATION

The motivation for preparation of a bill to be introduced in the Illinois General Assembly may come from many sources. A constituent may explain the need for a new law or an amendment of an existing statute to accomplish some purpose that he deems desirable; the constituent may be acting as an individual or he may represent an interest group or a local government. Another source of bills is the studies made by legislative commissions. A large number of bills

of Congress. Most congressional appropriations are the subject of permanent authorizations and are considered each year only by the Appropriations Committee. Some programs, however, receive only annual or biennial authorizations and must be reviewed every one or two years by a substantive legislative committee as well as the Appropriations Committee.

In the Illinois legislature there is no distinction between an authorization and an appropriation, nor is there a requirement for authorization by a substantive committee before funds for a program can be approved by the Appropriations Committee. The appropriations committees in the General Assembly normally are responsible for deciding upon the merits of a program and the funds needed to finance it, although fiscal decisions are seldom couched in programmatic terms. There are a few instances when bills are referred to a substantive committee before consideration by the Appropriations Committee. Even in these cases the responsibility for the entire spending decision rests with the Appropriations Committee.

are also prepared and introduced at the request of an agency of the state government.

Although a member is not required to prepare and introduce a bill at the request of a constituent, a reasonable request of this type is infrequently turned down. This relationship carries out the constitutional provision that "the people have the right . . . to make known their opinions to their representatives, and to apply for redress of grievances." The *Legislative Synopsis and Digest*, issued by the Legislative Reference Bureau, sometimes shows bills as being introduced "by request."

No set procedures are required for the preparation of a bill. Typically a member discusses the purposes and aims of the bill he wishes to introduce with the Legislative Reference Bureau. That agency, with its staff and legal draftsmen, then transfers the general ideas into a specific bill. In other cases, the legislator may actually make a rough draft of a bill himself and take it to the Reference Bureau before consulting with its staff.

Bills may be introduced in either house of the General Assembly, but only by a member or a committee of that house. A bill may be introduced and sponsored by a single member or several members. The names of the sponsors are listed on printed bills, in the journals, and in the *Digest*. Introduction of bills is discussed in detail later in this chapter.

Sometimes a bill is developed in discussions in a legislative committee, and in these cases the committee, rather than an individual member, is listed as the sponsor. These instances have been infrequent in the past, but have been increasing in recent years, particularly when the subject is complex, controversial, or highly political. A subcommittee or committee will often take some of the features of several bills referred to it and introduce a new bill. Committee sponsorship of bills has also increased because of legislative rules permitting only committee bills and bills implementing the state budget to bypass the Rules Committee if introduced during the even year.

Fiscal Notes

Both the statutes and the rules of the House of Representatives require under certain circumstances that fiscal notes be attached to bills affecting the state's revenues or expenditures. The Legislative Reference Bureau must make the following notation in a prominent place on any bill which it believes to fall within this category: "Fiscal Note Act may be applicable." The *Legislative Synopsis and Digest* must also carry a notation next to the entry for a particular bill to the effect that the bill may be subject to the fiscal note requirement, or that a fiscal note has been obtained by the sponsor.

There has been a tendency for the fiscal note procedure to be used as a dilatory tactic on the part of the opposition to a particular piece of legislation. The statute provides that "Every bill, except those bills making a direct appropriation, the purpose or effect of which is to expend any State funds or to increase or decrease the revenue of the State, either directly or indirectly, shall have prepared for it prior to second reading in the house of introduction a brief explanatory statement or note which shall include a reliable estimate of the anticipated change in State expenditures or revenues under its provisions." Amendments recommended by a committee, or amendments offered on the floor, if they propose to affect the cost or revenues of a measure substantially, are also subject to fiscal note requirements.

Primary responsibility for obtaining a fiscal note (if, for example, the Reference Bureau has indicated that one is necessary) rests with the sponsor of a bill. The sponsor must request from the state agency most directly concerned with the bill an estimate of its effect on expenditures or revenues. The agency is given five calendar days in which to reply; it may seek and be granted by the sponsor an extension of time not to extend beyond June 15 of the odd-numbered year following the date of the request.

If the sponsor decides that his bill needs no fiscal note, any member of either house may thereafter request that such a note be obtained. Even though the chair may rule one way or the other on the appropriateness of that request, a request of this nature will prevail if supported by a majority of those members present and voting in the house of which the sponsor is a member.

The agency preparing the fiscal note may not inject into it any comment or opinion on the merits of the bill, but technical or mechanical defects may be noted. Information concerning the bill and any fiscal note prepared for it must be considered as confidential until the bill is introduced.

Judicial Notes

Legislation adopted in 1969 requires a "judicial note" to be prepared for "every bill, the purpose and effect of which is to increase or decrease the number of appellate judges, circuit judges, associate circuit judges or magistrates in the State, either directly or indirectly. . . ." Such a note must also be prepared when any measure is amended to increase or decrease the number of judges.

The note is to be prepared by the director of the Administrative Office of the Illinois Courts upon request of the sponsor of the bill. "The note shall be factual in nature . . . and shall provide a reliable estimate of the need of a decrease or increase of judges or magistrates based upon population and case load, . . ." the statute directs. "If it is determined that such need can not be ascertained, the judicial note shall contain a statement to that effect. . . . No comment or opinion shall be included in the judicial note with regard to the merits of the measure. . . ."

A sponsor of a bill may be of the opinion that a judicial note is not required. In that case, "any member of either house may thereafter request that a note be obtained, and in such case the matter shall be decided by majority vote of those present and voting in the house of which he is a member." In practice, the judicial note is seldom used.

RESOLUTIONS AND MOTIONS

Although the General Assembly "acts" primarily by passing bills, it uses two other devices that give formal expression to its actions: resolutions and motions. Resolutions vary greatly in form and purpose. Those adopted by only one house for some purpose within that chamber are known as simple resolutions. Joint resolutions may be similar in purpose to simple resolutions, but they must be passed by both houses. At the beginning of each session much of the organization of each house — as well as the formal procedures attendant upon the opening day — are accomplished through the adoption of resolutions. For example, the rules of each house are adopted by simple resolution, and the participation of the two houses in the inauguration of state officers is facilitated by joint resolution. Resolutions are generally adopted by voice vote although occasionally a roll call may be requested. Unlike bills, they do not have to be read at large on three consecutive legislative days and are seldom referred to committee. The rules of each house require that resolutions be referred to the Executive Committee. However, in the House most resolutions are placed on the consent calendar, and in the Senate the vast majority are adopted promptly upon request of the sponsor for suspension of the rules and the immediate consideration of the resolution.

Joint resolutions proposing amendments to either the Illinois or U.S. constitutions or calling a constitutional convention are important exceptions to this customary procedure. The rules of the House require that resolutions proposing constitutional amendments must be specially designated, numbered, and listed separately on the calendar. Most importantly, by constitutional provision all proposed state constitutional amendments must be read in full on three separate legislative days in each house before the vote is taken on final passage. Both houses have adopted deadlines governing the introduction, consideration, and passage of proposed constitutional amendments. Resolutions proposing consitutional amendments must have a three-fifths majority of all members elected for passage, and, like all resolutions, do not require the approval of the governor.[7] Final approval of any change in the state constitution must come from the people in a statewide election next occurring at least six months after legislative approval. This means that during an even-numbered year the General Assembly must act affirmatively on the question of placing a proposed constitutional change before the people by the first Tuesday after the first Monday in May if that question is to appear on the November ballot that year.

From time to time the General Assembly notifies the U.S. Congress of its feeling on a particular issue by passing a joint resolution detailing its position on matters of national or international concern. This tradition of "memorializing" Congress is old and well estab-

[7] The majority necessary for ratification of a federal constitutional amendment could be changed by legislative rule to a simple majority (possibly only of those voting, a quorum being present), as the result of a federal district court opinion, although the rules of both houses of the 1975-76 General Assembly required a three-fifths majority. See Chapter 1, footnote 16.

lished, even though its purpose, according to one member of the General Assembly, has changed over the years: "Originally, up until early in this century, U.S. senators were chosen by the legislature so that when the legislature instructed a senator to vote for or against something or to introduce a bill along a certain line, this was followed closely by the members of the U.S. Senate. But the tradition of having these memorials has continued, even though to my knowledge they've really been just a waste of time. About the only thing that you get out of it is that it is journalized in the *Congressional Record.*"

In addition to facilitating organization and procedure, resolutions typically honor individuals for special achievements; offer condolences following the death of a member, former member, or a prominent citizen; or congratulate business, civic, or educational groups for contributions to the public service. Resolutions serve a variety of purposes, as one senator suggested while reminiscing about a former colleague:

> I can think of one member of the Senate who used to make a great thing every week of offering two or three congratulatory resolutions. Whatever it was, he was there with a resolution, and I think he really made some political mileage out of this. Protocol requires that these things never be turned down. You get a beautiful embossed copy in a folder with a red ribbon and a gold seal and the signature of the president of the Senate. If it's a joint resolution, it's got [the signatures of] not only the president and the secretary of the Senate but also the speaker and the clerk of the House. Normally you make an event of presenting it to the people involved, either to the coach of the team, or the debate coach, or the leader of the band. You might even call the local newspaper and get your picture in the paper. "Isn't it nice that the Illinois Senate took time from its busy schedule to honor our kids?" That's the value of a congratulatory resolution.

A motion is primarily a procedural tool. It may be presented orally (written out ahead of time) or in writing on demand of the presiding officer or any member. No second is required. A motion to take a bill out of committee (technically called "discharging the committee of further consideration of the bill") and bring it to the floor for consideration, or to refer it to another committee in opposition to the wishes of the committee then holding it, must be offered in writing. So must motions made with respect to bills returned by the governor. However, the familiar motions to reconsider an action, to recess, or to adjourn are usually offered orally, unless the period of adjournment would exceed three days and thus require joint action of both houses through use of a joint resolution.

As part of the language of parliamentary procedure, motions are important weapons on the floor of each chamber. The rules governing their use are found in the formal rules of each house and in *Robert's Rules of Order Newly Revised.* The obvious difference between a motion and a resolution is that the latter uses the word "resolved" in its acting or declaratory clause. One who offers a *resolution* ordinarily *moves* its adoption.

CALENDARS

Indispensable to an orderly legislative process are the calendars that are prepared each day by the secretary of the Senate and the clerk of the House and placed on each member's desk before the session begins. The calendars show at which order of business each bill is while it is before the full house.

Both the House and Senate calendars are similar, although the Senate rules make only passing reference to them. The House rules direct the clerk of the House to prepare a daily calendar "showing all special orders of the day and all bills and resolutions in their proper order of reading." All bills appear on the calendar in numerical order and are grouped according to the daily order of business. In the House the calendar also indicates the last day on which a bill can be acted on under House rules. The Senate calendar on a full day of activity groups bills being considered by the full body numerically in the following order: (1) Senate bills on second reading; (2) Senate bills on third reading; (3) House bills on third reading; (4) House bills on second reading; (5) House bills on first reading.

The Senate then normally considers each bill as it appears in this order on the calendar. The procedure in the House is somewhat similar except that the House calendar provides for several additional classifications. These include Senate bills on first reading — first legislative day, Senate bills on second reading — first legislative day, and House bills on second reading — first legislative day. The House calendar is, of course, arranged in the opposite order from that outlined above for the Senate. Bills in the House are also called in the order in which they appear on the calendar except that the speaker may call bills pertaining to the same subject for consideration at the same time, or he may, and frequently does, call bills in the order in which they will be tabled under the thirty-day rule. However, either body can proceed out of order to any order of business or return to any order already passed at any time by unanimous consent or on a motion adopted by a simple majority in either house. In the House the order of business can also be changed at any time by the speaker. For these reasons there are frequent deviations in the formal order of business during each day's session.

The sponsor of each bill is listed on the calendar along with a few words describing the bill.[8] Appropriation bills are printed in boldface type, and bills that have been amended are so designated by the letter "A" appearing after the bill's number. A list of committee hearings scheduled for that day is provided at the end of the calendar. In addition to bills at various stages of reading, the calendars list bills on postponed consideration, bills or resolutions on the speaker's table or the secretary's desk, and bills vetoed or returned by the governor. The House calendar also specifically identifies joint resolutions which propose amendments to either the state or federal constitutions.

The calendar used to be printed on one sheet and would grow in size as the session progressed until, in the closing days, it was often more than two yards square and listed several hundred bills. In recent years a change in the style of printing has resulted in the use of a pocket-size booklet format. These new calendars still con-

---

[8] The House calendars usually provide no more than an indication of which agency of government or which chapter in the statutes is affected; the Senate calendars usually carry the synopsis contained in the *Legislative Digest*. Hence, it is much easier to identify a particular bill on a Senate calendar than on a House calendar.

tain as many bills (or more), but they are much easier for a legislator to work with while seated at his or her desk on the floor. They also make it possible for a legislator or legislative observer to move around the statehouse with them in hand.

Consent Calendars

Both the House and Senate have experimented with the use of a timesaving device known as the consent calendar, which is printed as part of the regular daily calendar. First adopted by the Senate in 1969, this procedure allows noncontroversial bills and resolutions to traverse the legislative process without suffering from extended debate on each reading. Since 1973 only the House has used this procedure. Bills may be placed on the consent calendar by report of a standing committee upon the unanimous vote of the members present. No bill regarding any revenue or appropriations matter may be placed on the consent calendar.

The consent calendar used by the House during the past several years has consisted of two parts: consent calendar — second reading and consent calendar — third reading. A bill appearing in the first category must remain there for at least one legislative day. Thereafter it may be taken up during any daily session. No debate is permitted, although questions of the sponsor are. Only amendments adopted by the committee recommending the bill may be offered; these are adopted automatically on second reading. When a bill in this position is called, it is advanced to consent calendar — third reading unless the bill is objected to and removed from the consent calendar. A bill must spend at least three legislative days on this order of the consent calendar. A roll call vote is required on final passage and is taken on each eligible bill during the last daily session of each week.

Any bill on the consent calendar may be removed for the remainder of a session by written objection of any six members of the House, the sponsor of the bill, or any one or more members of a challenging committee composed of three members appointed by the speaker and three members appointed by the minority leader. A bill removed from the consent calendar goes on the daily calendar on the order of second reading of bills.

Special Orders

Special orders provide a means of deviating from a rigid application of the daily order, thus speeding the work on a particular bill or entire group of measures. The Committee on Rules in either house, being permitted to report at any time, may announce a special order of business for the consideration of particularly urgent items, and this order may be suspended, amended, or modified only by a constitutional majority on a roll call vote.

INTRODUCTION OF BILLS

As mentioned earlier, bills may originate in either house and must be introduced by members of the General Assembly. The chief sponsor of a bill may be joined in sponsorship by any number of his colleagues in the same chamber, although he retains primary responsibility for moving his bill through both houses. Thus each bill customarily has a number of sponsors even though it becomes identified with the chief sponsor, whose name appears first in the list of sponsors that heads each printed bill. In addition, the practice of having bills sponsored by committees is becoming more prevalent.

A 1961 act, as amended in 1967, makes it possible for members to prefile bills with the office of the secretary of the Senate or the clerk of the House between November 30 of an election year and the opening day of each new General Assembly. All prefiled bills are automatically introduced on opening day. Prefiling was originally intended to encourage early introduction of bills; however, during the present decade this practice has been used very little as the end of one legislative session has come closer and closer to the beginning of the next. Instead it has been used more for obtaining publicity for the sponsors during a period when legislative news is relatively light.

In 1967 the General Assembly passed legislation requiring that before introduction all bills be approved for form by the Legislative Reference Bureau. During recent years this has proved to be even more essential than it was previously because the bureau now has the entire set of statutes on a computer retrieval system. Annual spring and fall sessions have necessitated a continuous updating of the statutory base and review of pending legislation to make sure it conforms to the current base (which could likely be different from the latest set of printed statutes). After a bill receives the bureau's approval, the proper number of copies for introduction is turned over to the chief sponsor. The bill is submitted in this form to the clerk of the House or the secretary of the Senate with the names of all the sponsors written on the cover sheet of the original type-written bill.[9] The clerk or the secretary assigns each bill a number as the bills are formally introduced at the proper point in the daily order of business.

COMMITTEE ACTION

As each bill is introduced and given a number, it is read by title, ordered printed, and referred to committee. As mentioned in Chapter 2, both House and Senate rules require that in even-numbered years all bills other than budget or committee bills be referred directly to the Rules Committee. In these cases the bills are introduced and assigned numbers, but they are not read a first time or ordered printed unless and until the Rules Committee reports them out favorably. Committee referral is the daily responsibility in either house of the Committee on Assignment of Bills.[10] Occasionally a noncontroversial bill will be advanced to second reading without reference to committee, but with each session this is occurring less and less.[11]

After a bill is assigned to a standing committee, legislative norms make it the responsibility of the sponsor to request the committee

[9] As a bill clears each successive hurdle in the legislative process, the clerk or the secretary notes on the original typewritten copy of the bill the date and the action taken. The original bill constitutes an important part of the public record on legislation, and it remains in the possession of the clerk or secretary in the house of origin except during the period of committee consideration. When a bill is passed, the engrossed copy is sent to the second house where the printer works from this copy rather than the original bill. After each session, the original copy of each bill is sent to the secretary of state for deposit in the State Archives.

[10] Day-to-day responsibility for bill referrals almost always falls to the chairman of the Committee on the Assignment of Bills. The full committee rarely meets to assign bills.

[11] The House rules now require an affirmative vote of at least 107 members to use this procedure. The procedure for advancing bills without reference is described in Chapter 4.

chairman to set his bill for hearing. House rules, however, require a committee chairman to set a bill within thirty days of its assignment to his committee. They also require a chairman, should he fail to set a bill within this time period, to post, hear, and take a vote on that bill no later than the last committee meeting prior to the forty-fifth day after its assignment. The setting of appropriation bills is largely a decision made by the chairman of the Appropriations Committee after consultation with the spokesman for the minority party on that committee. As the deadlines for reporting bills out of committee approach, other committee chairmen may also begin to balance the committee's workload by deciding which bills to set. In almost any case, a sponsor is still able to keep a bill from being heard before such time as he or she desires. As noted in Chapter 1, every committee, joint committee, and legislative commission is mandated by the constitution to give reasonable public notice prior to any of its meetings, including a statement of subjects to be considered. The rules of both houses provide for compliance with this requirement: in the Senate advance notice of a committee meeting must be given at least six days prior to that meeting, and in the House six and one-half days' notice is required.

All meetings of committees, joint committees, and commissions are open to the public unless specifically closed by a vote of two-thirds of the members elected to that house in the case of committees, or both houses in the case of joint committees and commissions. Committee members must be present to vote since proxy voting is no longer permitted in either house. Final committee reports consist only of the votes and the recommendation that the bill: (1) "do pass"; (2) "do not pass"; (3) "do pass as amended"; (4) "do not pass as amended" (House only); (5) "do pass and be placed upon the consent calendar" (House only); (6) "do pass as amended and be placed upon the consent calendar" (House only); (7) be replaced by a substitute bill; or (8) be sent to the full body "without recommendation" (Senate only). In the Senate a bill is automatically reported out of committee with a "do not pass" recommendation unless it is set for a hearing within sixty days of assignment. If this happens, the bill is automatically tabled, unless a motion to recommit the bill to committee is supported by a majority of all the senators elected. A bill which has not received final committee action within forty-five days of assignment to a House committee is automatically tabled by rule except in the case of appropriation bills. A bill assigned to a House committee which is not reported out within forty-five days can avoid this fate if, prior to the expiration of the forty-five days, two-thirds of the committee members vote to place the bill on the committee's interim study calendar.

FLOOR ACTION

If after committee consideration a bill is favorably reported, it will appear on the printed calendar the next day on the order of second reading in the Senate or second reading — first legislative day in the House. Any time after this, the sponsor may request at the appropriate moment that his bill be called for reading a second time and advanced to third reading, except in the House where a bill must remain on second reading for at least one day before it can be called. As discussed in the next section, any amendments must be offered on second reading. Near the end of the session unanimous consent is frequently given to advance a bill to third reading with the understanding that the sponsor will return the bill to second reading at a later time for consideration of any amendments. This can save a legislative day, which is quite important in the crush that comes during the final week of each session. In the House the speaker may call bills by subject, in the order in which they will be tabled under the thirty-day rule, or in numerical order. The Senate, a much smaller body, operates in a more informal manner. There the president will normally proceed down the calendar in numerical order and ask the sponsor if he or she desires to have a particular bill called. A proper nod of the head and the secretary will read the bill by title.

Amendments

By rule, bills may be amended only on second reading.[12] Amendments recommended for adoption by a committee are considered first, and then amendments may be offered from the floor, as they

---

[12] Amendments added in the house of origin receive only five of the six required legislative days of reading. (Three days are required in each house, but a bill passed by one house can be read in the second chamber on the same

often are. A voice vote is customarily employed for each amendment unless a roll call vote is requested by a member. Amendments that have been adopted to House and Senate bills must be printed and placed on each member's desk at least one day before the bill can be considered on third reading. In the House, committee amendments must be printed before they can be considered on second reading. There is no comparable Senate rule, although at the request of five senators amendments must be ordered printed prior to being voted on.[13]

Debate

In general there is a relaxed attitude about the rules and procedures to limit debate on measures until the last two or three weeks of a session. However, assuming that proponents and opponents of each measure are given an equal opportunity to be heard, there are rules

---

day. Thus the minimum time for passage is five days after introduction.) Amended bills adopted in the second house receive only two readings in that house and only one in the chamber of origin on a concurrence vote. Does the three-reading requirement apply to the amended version as well as the original? Judicial construction clearly indicates that the three-reading requirement does not apply where the amendment is germane to the original bill (*People* v. *Lewis,* 5 Ill. 2d 117, 125 N.E.2d 87 (1955); *People* v. *Hightower,* 414 Ill. 537, 112 N.E.2d 126 (1953); *People* ex rel. *Sellers* v. *Brady,* 262 Ill. 578, 105 N.E. 1 (1914)). There has been only one case in Illinois in which a bill has been invalidated by the courts because the amendments were not germane and the bill had consequently failed to meet the three-reading requirement. In this instance, the original bill had been completely changed when the title was amended and everything after the enacting clause stricken and new provisions substituted (*Giebelhausen* v. *Daley,* 407 Ill. 25, 95 N.E.2d 84 (1950)). In September 1972 the governor vetoed H.B. 1954 on the advice of the attorney general because "the substance of this enactment was achieved only in the final hours of the spring legislative session in the adoption of a second conference committee report. . . . As the report of the Attorney General evidences, the conference committee report adopted in the two houses was a flagrant violation of the germaneness rule which I am constitutionally bound to both note and reject." The attorney general also noted that "by virtue of the 'enrolled bill rule,' an allegation that a bill was passed in violation of a constitutionally required procedure must be proven by reference to the face of the bill itself." See the governor's veto message of September 8, 1972, to the House of Representatives *re* House Bill 1954, 1971-72 General Assembly. In practice, substantial changes are made at the amendment stage, and if the amendment is at all relevant to the original bill, it is unlikely that a successful challenge can be made in the courts on the three-reading requirement once the presiding officers of each house place their signatures upon the enrolled bill.

[13] In recent sessions the presiding officer of the Senate has ruled that amendments reproduced by a photocopy method meet this requirement.

that may be invoked on any question to limit excessive speaking or even a filibuster. The rules of the two houses are somewhat different.

In the House of Representatives no member may speak longer than ten minutes at one time, nor more than once on the same question unless leave is granted by the House — usually unanimous consent is required. Late in the session, unanimous consent may be hard to obtain. An exception to the ten-minute rule is made for the sponsor of a bill, who has five additional minutes to close the debate. In addition to the time given for general debate, each member of the House is allowed two minutes to explain his vote during the roll call.

In the Senate, no member may speak longer than five minutes without consent at any one time, nor more than twice on the same question, and the second opportunity is afforded only after all other senators have had an opportunity to speak. If one senator asks a question of another, the latter's answer is charged against the former's time. As in the House the sponsor is reserved the right to close the debate. If a senator wants to "explain his vote" he must do so during general debate since explanations of votes on roll call are now prohibited.

Each house permits closure of debate by use of the motion calling for the "previous question," which has the effect, if voted affirmatively, of causing the debate to cease so as to dispose of the question. If such a motion is successful, the sponsor is still entitled to close the debate, after which the vote on the question before the body is taken. It has been the practice of the Senate president to permit any senator who had sought recognition prior to the putting of a successful "previous question" motion to speak before allowing the sponsor to close debate. In the House the closing of debate does not impair a member's right to explain his vote on roll call.

Time allowed for debating or explaining one's vote may be restricted near the end of the session by adopting a resolution or amending the rules to allow less time for these steps. As Professor John Wahlke has observed: "With respect to legislatures, it is fairly obvious that a body of several hundred persons can discuss any matter only if almost every member agrees to say almost nothing. It is less obvious, but equally important, that personal and informal methods of dealing with its business are more possible for small than for large groups."[14] This helps to explain why limiting debate does not necessarily restrict members of either house if they wish to engage in stalling tactics. By offering a series of amendments, requesting verification of votes, and using other procedural devices, a relatively small group of legislators can tie up the business of either house for considerable periods of time.

Roll Call Vote

Passage on third reading is by roll call vote and requires a majority of the members elected — eighty-nine in the House and thirty in the Senate. Vacancies caused by death or other reasons do not change the required majority and an absence or a vacancy becomes, in effect, a no vote. As a consequence, especially on controversial bills, it may become important to have all supporters or all opponents in their seats and voting. Each vote is recorded in the journal.

The new constitution provides that vacancies are to be filled by appointment within thirty days after a vacancy occurs. Legislation implementing this provision was approved in 1973, making the district party legislative committee the appointing authority. During the next three years three vacancies in the Senate and eleven in the House were filled pursuant to that legislation. As required by the constitution, the law provides that an appointee must be a member of the same political party as the person he succeeds, and that the appointment shall be for the remainder of the term unless, in the case of a Senate vacancy, more than twenty-eight months remain in the term, in which case the appointed senator serves only until the next general election.

The constitutional requirement for a record roll call vote on final passage results in an impressive number of roll calls each session. By the time the 1973-74 General Assembly adjourned *sine die* on January 8, 1975, 1,561 bills had passed both houses. In the two chambers combined, then, there were, at the very minimum, well over three thousand roll call votes. This figure does not take into account frequent roll call votes on amendments and procedural motions or bills defeated on third reading. The General Assembly obviously devotes a significant portion of its energies to the simple

[14] John C. Wahlke, "Organization and Procedure," in *State Legislatures in American Politics,* p. 132.

act of voting. In contrast, roll calls in the Congress, where there is no constitutional mandate for them, are far less frequent. During the same period, for example, there were fewer than seven hundred roll call votes in both chambers of that body.

The unavoidable burden of roll calls in the General Assembly is now eased in both houses by the use of an electronic voting machine in each chamber. While the House has had this equipment for some time, the Senate did not acquire electronic voting until 1974. An oral roll call taken by the clerk or secretary, who called each member's name and recorded his vote manually, was an extremely time-consuming chore in the days before the use of electronic assistance. Now each representative or senator has a voting box located on the top of his or her desk. When the presiding officer directs the clerk or secretary to take the roll, each member has a brief period in which to push the yea, nay, or present button. Two large panels at the front of the chamber allow all those present to see how the entire membership is voting. A bright green light opposite a member's name indicates a yes vote, a red light no, while an amber light means present but not voting. The number of the bill or resolution being voted upon appears at the top of each panel. Directly below, the result of the vote is indicated in green, red, and amber lights. While the vote is being flashed on the large panels, the machine also records each member's vote on a printed form, providing the clerk or secretary with a permanent record of the vote seconds after it is taken.[15]

Consideration Postponed and Reconsideration

Any time before the final vote is announced by the presiding officer, the sponsor may move to postpone consideration of his bill if it appears the bill will be voted down. This motion puts the bill on the calendar on the order of consideration postponed and gives the sponsor time to work out any objections. It is also quite common on controversial bills for the proponents or opponents to "lock a bill in" by moving for reconsideration of the vote by which the bill

[15] After its voting machine was installed, the Senate adopted substantially tighter rules than the House has employed with respect to voting. In the upper chamber no member is permitted to vote after the machine is closed, even with unanimous consent. If a member is unable to get back to his desk in time to vote, he may journalize how he would have voted, but the secretary is not permitted to make any changes in the machine roll call.

passed or was defeated. The sponsor or a sympathetic colleague will then move to table the motion for reconsideration. The tabling motion is usually carried by the same vote that supported the original decision. Once the motion to reconsider is tabled, the vote on third reading is final and cannot be considered again. This procedure prevents opponents from getting a member who voted with the prevailing side to reverse his position and move for reconsideration of the final vote under more favorable conditions. If this procedure is not followed, and a member wishes to reopen the question, a member who voted on the prevailing side must move to reconsider within the next legislative day and while the bill or resolution involved is still in the custody of that house.

Second House Action

After a favorable vote on third reading, the bill is sent by the clerk or the secretary to his counterpart in the other chamber with a message stating that the bill has been passed. The membership is then informed and the bill is read by title, ordered printed, and placed on the order of first reading. In the case of nonbudgetary bills in even-year sessions the bill is first sent to the Rules Committee. In the latter case, a bill must clear the Rules Committee before it can make its way to first reading. After being read a first time the bill is assigned to a substantive committee and the path to final passage parallels the steps outlined above.

CONFERENCE COMMITTEES

Each house must approve amendments adopted in the other chamber. Otherwise a conference committee is appointed to work out differences of opinion.[16] After House passage of a Senate bill, for example, the clerk will send a message to the Senate asking for concurrence in House amendments to the bill. The secretary of the Senate then notifies the Senate and places the bill on the calendar as a special order of business. The Senate sponsor of the bill will move that the Senate concur or nonconcur in the House amendments. If the Senate agrees to the House amendments, passage is final and the bill goes to the governor. However, if the Senate fails

---

[16] Conference committees are discussed in more detail in Chapter 4.

to concur in the House action, a message is sent back to the House asking it to recede from its amendments. If the House does not recede, the Senate sponsor requests that the bill go to a conference committee consisting usually of five members from each house.

Only the subject of a disagreement is considered by a conference committee. Moreover, no subject matter is to be included in a conference report on an appropriation bill unless the subject matter directly relates to "matters of differences" and has been specifically referred to the conference committee.

If a conference committee fails to find any formula for agreement and so reports, a second conference committee may be appointed. Membership of the second conference committee may or may not be the same as the first.

Both the House and the Senate must approve the recommendations of the conference committee; otherwise the bill is lost since a bill must be passed by both houses in identical form. Each concurrence vote is equivalent to a vote on final passage, so it requires a majority of the members elected voting for the report, or a three-fifths majority if taken after June 30, if a long delay in the effective date is to be avoided.

A bill that passes both houses must be typed and transcribed in the house of origin, and amendments adopted in the second house are then incorporated into the bill. The clerk of the House or the secretary of the Senate certifies the bill, which must then be signed by the speaker of the House and the president of the Senate before presentation to the governor.[17]

GUBERNATORIAL ACTION[18]

The constitutional power of the governor to veto legislation passed by the General Assembly has always been a critical element in the

[17] The new state constitution provides in part that "the Speaker of the House of Representatives and the President of the Senate shall sign each bill that passes both houses to certify that the procedural requirements for passage have been met." This is the basis for the "enrolled bill rule" referred to above in footnote 12.

[18] The assistance of research by Raymond Coyne in the development of the following section is gratefully acknowledged. See his paper "Gubernatorial Powers," presented at the annual meeting of the Midwest Political Science Association, Chicago, Illinois, May 3-5, 1973, pp. 30-45.

legislative process. As one commentator suggested several years ago, "The governor stands at the center of the arena as chief executive and chief legislator. . . ."[19] Although students of Illinois politics generally advocate a strong executive, they also seek a strong legislature. These goals "are not mutually exclusive," although they may necessarily conflict at times.[20]

The members of the Sixth Illinois Constitutional Convention evidently agreed with this assessment of the relationship between the chief executive and legislature. One of the delegates, in an article published prior to the convention, noted: "In Illinois the governor's veto is virtually absolute, and the question is whether it is desirable to leave it that way. Knowledge of the finality of the governor's action may lessen the legislature's acceptance of responsibility for its action; if so, that may be a serious impediment to the development of a strong legislative branch — which is equally a goal of constitutional revision."[21]

In the convention itself it appears that most of the delegates subscribed to the view that it was time for the legislature to stop taking a "back seat" to the governor. The majority of the Committee on the Legislative Article, in explaining their proposal to the entire convention, argued as if they believed that the balance of power was unbalanced and that it was desirable to expand the potential power of the General Assembly: "Every effort must be made . . . to restore a proper balance of power in our tri-partite separation of powers among the executive, legislative and judicial branches, and this provision represents at least a small opportunity to place confidence in the General Assembly. . . ."[22]

[19] James B. Holderman, "The Modern Governor: Limits of Effectiveness," in *The Office of Governor*, Final Report and Background Papers, Assembly on the Office of Governor (Urbana: Institute of Government and Public Affairs, University of Illinois, 1963), p. 49.

[20] In addition to the papers of the Assembly on the Office of Governor cited above, see David Kenney, *Basic Illinois Government: A Systematic Explanation*, rev. ed. (Carbondale: Southern Illinois University Press, 1974), pp. 241-46; Dawn Clark Netsch, "The Governor Shall . . . ; Observations on the Executive Article of the Illinois Constitution," *Chicago Bar Record* 50 (October 1968): 28-36; and William S. Hanley, "The 1970 Constitution and the Executive Veto," *Public Affairs Bulletin* 1 (January-April 1972).

[21] Netsch, "The Governor Shall," p. 34.

[22] Illinois, Sixth Constitutional Convention, *Record of Proceedings, Committee Proposals* (Springfield, 1972), Legislative Committee Proposal 1, VI:1367.

In the end, the constitutional framers broadened the governor's powers while at the same time they lowered the numerical requirement for overruling the governor. Formerly, when a bill passed by the General Assembly was presented to the governor, he had three choices in every case except appropriation bills. He could approve it, veto it, or allow it to become law without his signature. In the case of appropriation bills he had the additional option of an item veto. Under the new constitution the governor retains all of these options while acquiring two more. At the same time the vote required to override a gubernatorial veto is now a three-fifths majority rather than two-thirds.

Item-Reduction Veto

The Con-Con delegates expanded the governor's "fine-tuning" control over the "throttle" of state expenditures by giving him an item-reduction veto power subject to a legislative override by a simple majority vote. The line-item veto, subject to the regular three-fifths majority needed to override, was retained in the document. In recommending the proposed reduction veto to the entire convention, the Committee on the Executive argued: "Modern appropriation practices have rendered the existing item veto virtually obsolete because it is no longer common to have appropriation bills so detailed that a veto could strike an entire item without being destructive of the program of the agency."[23]

Thus, the convention reversed a landmark 1915 Illinois Supreme Court decision[24] so as to "revitalize the intent of the 1884 addition to the constitution of the item veto."[25] With this change the governor is no longer faced with the necessity of accepting or rejecting an appropriated amount in toto. A line-item reduction veto may be restored to its original amount by a record vote of a majority of the members elected to each house.

After the new constitution went into effect, Governor Richard Ogilvie wasted little time applying this new authority. On July 13, 1971, twelve days after the constitution's effective date, he used

[23] Ibid., Executive Committee Proposal 1, VI:401.
[24] *Fergus* v. *Russell*, 270 Ill. 304, 110 N.E. 130 (1915).
[25] Illinois, Sixth Constitutional Convention, *Record of Proceedings, Committee Proposals*, Executive Committee Proposal 1, VI:401.

this power in reviewing appropriation bills passed by the General Assembly for fiscal year 1972. By the time he had finished acting on these bills, the governor had reduced the 141 line items in sixteen bills for total reductions of $146,253,791. Despite this unprecedented cut in appropriations for a single fiscal year, and the fact that only a simple majority was needed to restore the original amounts, the governor's actions held in every case.[26] Following the 1974 session, Governor Daniel Walker used this device to remove an entire series of "retirement amendments" which provided for a higher level of funding state pension systems than the governor had recommended. As a result he exercised his item-reduction veto in signing forty-four bills, and his line-item veto as well as the reduction veto on another twenty-six bills. This pattern was continued in 1975, when the governor reduced the appropriations in forty bills and used his line-item veto together with his reduction veto on an additional eighteen bills.

Amendatory Veto

The delegates also added "a flexible tool of government to be used by both the lawmakers and the governor"[27] which is commonly referred to as an amendatory veto. Instead of having to either approve or veto a bill in its entirety, the governor may now return a bill with specific recommendations for change to the house in which it originated. These specific recommendations for change may be accepted by a vote of the majority of the elected members of each house. The legislature also has the option of overriding an amendatory veto, as it has for any kind of veto. Such bills in which gubernatorial changes are accepted by the General Assembly must be presented again to the governor for his certification that the final products conform with his recommendations, whereupon they become law. If the governor refuses to certify a bill, he returns it to the originating house as a vetoed bill.

The amendatory veto was designed to save time and money while enabling state government to function more smoothly, more effi-

[26] Hanley, "The 1970 Constitution."
[27] Joseph A. Tecson, chairman, Committee on the Executive, Sixth Illinois Constitutional Convention, "Separation of Powers," letter to the editor, *Chicago Tribune,* February 24, 1972.

ciently, and more effectively.[28] As one delegate explained: "It is not our intention to change the separation of powers with respect to the Legislative Article. It is to make certain that it remains historically the way we now understand it to be."[29] Thus, it appears the amendatory veto was designed to add to the power of both the governor and the General Assembly without changing the balance of power between them.

Yet, this new gubernatorial power has already evoked considerable controversy centering on the question of how much flexibility the delegates intended the governor to have in making changes in legislation presented for his signature.[30] Many an incumbent legislator might attribute the adage "the road to hell is paved with good intentions" to the amendatory veto. It has been charged with upsetting the balance of power between the two branches of government, destroying the viability of the separation of powers, and enabling the governor to dominate the legislative process. There are also those who believe the problem has been caused by the way individual governors have used the amendatory veto rather than the veto authority itself. The central question in this controversy has been whether it was intended that this veto be used by the governor to change only technical errors or whether he was meant to be able to go so far as to completely strike the substance of the bill presented to him and substitute an entirely new bill.

At the time the new constitution went into effect, the Senate minority leader, a member of the same party as the governor, was among the first to voice concern about the possible weakening of the legislature vis-à-vis the governor due to the amendatory veto. Fearing "the General Assembly would be hamstrung by a Governor who could force absolute acceptance or rejection of totally new legislation," he sought clarification from the attorney general on how far the legislature could go in modifying the governor's recommendations.[31]

[28] Opinion of Attorney General William J. Scott to the Honorable W. Russell Arrington, File No. S-357, October 11, 1971.
[29] Mary A. Pappas, constitutional convention delegate, letter to the editor, *Chicago Tribune,* February 25, 1972.
[30] See, for example, Hanley, "The 1970 Constitution."
[31] Letter from Senate Minority Leader W. Russell Arrington to Attorney General William J. Scott, September 16, 1971.

In the opinion that resulted from that request the attorney general noted:

> It is evident that the Constitutional Convention intended to substitute for the old restricted veto power a plan under which legislation could be changed to the satisfaction of both the General Assembly and the Governor and could be upheld. Such a plan is practical, constructive, progressive and modern and could prove of inestimable value to the State in savings of time and costs. Such worthwhile objectives should not be thwarted by an interpretation which puts both the Governor and the General Assembly in a straight jacket [*sic*] of word definitions.[32]

The leader who requested the opinion, a former president pro tempore of the Senate, viewed the opinion as "a reaffirmation of the separation of powers in Illinois government."[33]

The speaker of the House of Representatives did not share the same concerns: "I don't buy the argument that the legislative process is being usurped. This amendatory veto is really a device to give legislation that would otherwise be vetoed a second life. It's like a window into the Governor's mind."[34]

Nevertheless, before the legislature's first experience with the amendatory veto ended, two joint resolutions proposing a constitutional amendment limiting the amendatory veto power had been introduced in the Senate. Those particular resolutions died with the end of the biennium, but in 1973 the General Assembly did approve House Joint Resolution Constitutional Amendment No. 7, which put the question of whether to limit the scope of the amendatory veto before the voters in the 1974 general election. The proposed amendment would have changed the first sentence of Article IV, section 9(e), of the constitution, which reads, "The Governor may return a bill together with specific recommendations for change to the house in which it originated"; the words "specific recommendations for the correction of technical errors or matters of form" would have replaced the words "specific recommendations for change."

[32] Opinion of the Attorney General, File No. S-357, October 11, 1971.
[33] Senate Minority Leader W. Russell Arrington, press release dated October 11, 1971.
[34] House Speaker W. Robert Blair, quoted by Tom Laue, "Chicago Democrat Offers Resolution to Abolish Amendatory Veto of Bills," Springfield *Illinois State Register,* October 19, 1971.

The proposed amendment cleared both houses by large margins (142 to 6 in the House; 52 to 4 in the Senate), but in the absence of an organized campaign in favor of ratification it is not surprising that the voters rejected the measure. The major argument in favor of the amendment was that the amendatory veto gives the governor too much power and amounts to a distortion of the normal legislative process; the argument against (and in favor of retention of the amendatory veto) was the value of the flexibility it affords and also the fact that the General Assembly can always decline to accept the governor's changes if it feels he has gone too far.[35]

Between January 6, 1971, and July 2, 1975, three general assemblies passed and sent to two governors of opposite parties 5,996 bills. Of these 633 (10.6 percent) were vetoed in their entirety, 23 (0.4 percent) were vetoed in part, 56 (0.9 percent) were vetoed in part and had appropriations reduced, 115 (1.9 percent) had appropriations reduced, and 198 (3.3 percent) were returned to the legislature with specific recommendations for change. Of the 198 amendatory vetoes during this period, the General Assembly accepted 150 proposed changes, which were then certified by the governor as conforming with his suggested changes. Forty-one amendatory vetoes were rejected, six were overriden, and one bill was declared law without further action. These 198 amendatory vetoes represented 19.2 percent of the total 1,025 bills vetoed during this period; 61.8 percent (633 bills) were vetoed outright; 11.2 percent (115 bills) had a line-item appropriation reduced; 2.3 percent (23 bills) received an item veto of an appropriation; and 5.5 percent (56 bills) contained both reduction and line-item vetoes in the same bill.

A study of the 198 bills which governors Ogilvie and Walker returned to the General Assembly by means of an amendatory veto during the first five years it was constitutionally permitted (1971-75) shows that most of these bills concerned general policy. With one exception, it was on this group of amendatory vetoes that the legislature failed to accept the governor's recommendations or overrode the veto. Of the 141 bills which were returned on policy grounds,

[35] Illinois Legislative Council, "Proposal to Limit the Amendatory Veto," ILC File 8-448 (June 12, 1974). The proposed constitutional amendment was defeated at the polls by 1,329,719 "no" votes to 1,302,313 "yes" votes.

40 were rejected or never returned to the governor, 4 were sent back to the governor with substitute amendments for his recommended changes, 6 were overridden, and 1 was declared law by the Senate president.

The changes which were made by the governor in the other fifty-seven bills which were returned for reasons other than general policy were all accepted by the General Assembly, except for one bill which was returned with a substantive drafting problem. The reasons for which these bills were returned included constitutional grounds (five bills), conflicts with other bills (twelve bills), substantive drafting problems (thirty-one bills), and minor drafting problems (eight bills).[36]

By means of contrast, during the eleven biennial sessions of the General Assembly held between 1949 and 1969, 2,262 (13.5 percent) of the 16,747 bills sent to the governor for approval were vetoed outright. This twenty-two-year average on the percentage of bills vetoed in their entirety by the governor is approximately 50 percent greater than the comparable percentage for the 1971-72 and the 1973-74 biennia. When 1975, the first year of the 1975-76 General Assembly, is included, however, this average is only 27 percent greater than the more recent five-year average. Also, when all forms of vetoes are taken into account, 17.1 percent of the bills passed by the General Assembly from 1971 through 1975 were not signed by the governor in the exact form in which he received them.

That this difference can be attributed in part to the changes in the constitutional role of the governor in the legislative process brought about by the 1970 constitution ought not to be denied. In a study of the governor's veto messages after the 1963 session, the Illinois Legislative Council found that 40 percent of the vetoes were based upon technical or nonsubstantive, rather than policy or constitutional, considerations. In a similar study made after the 1971 regular session, the governor's legislative counsel found that almost the same percentage (37.8 percent) of the vetoes that year were for technical reasons. For example, 35 (14.6 percent) of the 240 bills vetoed after the 1963 session were identical to others that were

[36] Data compiled by the authors, using figures from Illinois Legislative Council, "Proposal to Limit the Amendatory Veto," and Hanley, "The 1970 Constitution," for earlier years.

approved, and another 31 (12.9 percent) were duplicated in substance by still other bills. The percentages of bills vetoed after the 1971 session for these same reasons are only slightly less: 30 (13.4 percent) of the 225 bills vetoed that year were identical bills while another 28 (12.4 percent) were substantive duplicates. The only difference between the two years is that for 1971 7 of the duplicate bills (3.1 percent) were vetoed because their provisions were incorporated by executive amendment into another bill.[37]

Policy vetoes and other vetoes come within the personal discretion of the governor. In carrying out this responsibility the governor has come to rely upon the attorney general, the various code departments within the executive branch, and his own personal staff.

Despite the failure of the 1974 referendum, the use of the amendatory veto has been restricted somewhat by a 1972 Illinois Supreme Court decision which held that the governor may not use this power to substitute in form and substance completely new bills.[38] It is interesting to note, however, that in the first session after the defeat of the proposed constitutional amendment the governor returned 79 bills to the General Assembly. This compares with a total of 119 amendatory vetoes in all of the preceding four years.

Although the governor has gained significant new authority and flexibility in dealing with legislation passed by the General Assembly, the legislative branch has also gained added power in the dynamic relationship between two branches of state government. Because the General Assembly usually passed most of its legislation during the last month of the session and then adjourned *sine die*, almost invariably the governor's action was final; the legislature rarely had any further opportunity to challenge his decision. The old constitutional requirement that a two-thirds majority of the members elected was necessary to override the governor also contributed to the finality of his veto. The close partisan division in the House resulting from the cumulative voting system made it difficult, if not impossible, to muster the required majority since the governor needed only to secure the support of a portion of his party to sustain his veto.

[37] Hanley, "The 1970 Constitution." Hanley's figures for 1963 are taken from Illinois Legislative Council, "Executive Vetoes after Adjournment of the Legislature," ILC File 5-034 (May 1964).
[38] *People* ex rel. *Klinger* v. *Howlett*, 50 Ill. 2d 242, 278 N.E.2d 84 (1972).

As mentioned earlier, under the new constitution the majority needed to override has been relaxed from two-thirds to three-fifths. Thus, although it remains difficult to override the governor's veto, it is no longer virtually impossible, particularly now that the legislature is in session more often. In January 1972, for example, the General Assembly successfully overrode the governor twice in one day. This set the trend for an increasing number of successful overrides in each succeeding year, with three overrides in 1972, five in 1973, thirteen in 1974, and seventeen in 1975. This is in sharp contrast to the history of legislative attempts to override the governor under the 1870 constitution. During the one-hundred-year life span of the old constitution, gubernatorial vetoes were successfully challenged on only four occasions — in 1871, 1895, 1936, and 1969.[39]

Presentation of Bills

Besides widening the governor's veto powers and lowering the numerical requirement for overriding a veto, the new constitution deals with several other questions affecting the executive's consideration of enacted bills. The 1870 constitution failed to fix a period within which bills had to be presented to the governor. As a result, during the past three decades the enrolling and engrossing committees of each house spaced their presentation of bills over a substantial period following adjournment.[40] The old constitution was also silent on the question of when the General Assembly was required to consider the veto messages of the governor. This allowed the 1967-68 General Assembly, for example, to override a gubernatorial veto of a legislative pay raise only an hour before the convening of the 1969-70 General Assembly. A third problem under the 1870 document was the inadequacy of the absolute ten-day period given to the governor for his consideration of a bill once it was presented to him. The governor either took action on a bill

[39] Hanley, "The 1970 Constitution."
[40] In *People* ex rel. *Peterson* v. *Hughes,* 372 Ill. 602, 25 N.E.2d 75 (1939), and *People* ex rel. *Erskine* v. *Hughes,* 373 Ill. 144, 25 N.E.2d 801 (1940), the Illinois Supreme Court held that the General Assembly had the power to determine when a bill would be presented to the governor and that (under the 1870 constitution) it was the day of presentation that fixed the beginning of the ten-day period in which the governor had to act even though this might be weeks after both enactment and adjournment.

within this period or watched it become law without his consideration.

In response to these problems, the new state charter provides a specific period of presentation (thirty calendar days after passage) which is judicially enforceable; allows the governor sixty calendar days in which to act on a bill after it is presented to him and after which it becomes law without his signature; and requires each house of the General Assembly to act within fifteen calendar days after its receipt of the governor's message, thereby insuring an ultimate terminal date for final consideration of any bill. The new constitution further stipulates that if the recess or adjournment of the General Assembly prevents the return of a bill within the sixty-day period, the bill and the governor's objections are to be filed with the secretary of state's office. The secretary of state is then compelled to return the bill and objections to the originating house "promptly upon the next meeting of the same General Assembly," when the governor's objections shall immediately be entered upon its journal.

Public Act Numbers

If a bill is approved or certified by the governor, or passed by the General Assembly over the governor's veto, it is then assigned an official act number in addition to its bill number. These act numbers provide precise identification and simplify citation. Each biennium in which the General Assembly meets is identified by number. For example, the 1975-76 General Assembly is also known as the Seventy-ninth General Assembly. The General Assembly which enacts the law is indicated by the first two numbers, followed by a dash and the numerical order of the governor's approval. Thus, P.A. 79-10 indicates that the act has been passed by the Seventy-ninth General Assembly and that it is the tenth bill signed into law by the governor during that biennium.

EFFECTIVE DATES

Determining the effective date of a bill used to be an easy matter. Under the 1870 constitution every bill passed by the General Assembly became effective on July 1 following passage. Court interpretation of "passage" to mean final action taken by the two houses of the legislature, and not the action of the governor, expanded this rule to mean July 1 or upon becoming law, whichever was later. Bills which were accompanied by an emergency clause and passed by a two-thirds majority became effective when signed by the governor. As noted earlier, this latter requirement served to impose a June 30 deadline on a legislative session since it was nearly impossible to obtain that large a majority on anything but a bill which was agreed upon in advance by both sides.

The new constitution still distinguishes between bills passed prior to July 1 and bills passed after June 30 except that the legal rules applicable to each group have changed. Pursuant to a constitutional mandate, the General Assembly in 1971 provided that October 1 was to be the uniform effective date for laws passed prior to July 1 unless the law specifically provided otherwise. This was to allow at least ninety days for a law to be printed and made available to the public before it took effect. This, of course, has meant that every appropriation bill and every other bill which the General Assembly wants to take effect upon its becoming law must specifically provide for a different effective date. Any bill which is passed between July 1 and December 30 becomes effective on July 1 of the next calendar year unless the General Assembly by a three-fifths majority in each house provides for an earlier effective date.

These parameters are relatively simple to apply as long as the necessary section specifically providing for an effective date is inserted whenever it is either necessary or desired. The matter was complicated by the Illinois Supreme Court ruling in *People* ex rel. *Klinger* that these are not the only limits. Defining final passage to be the vote by which both houses on October 28, 1971, accepted the governor's specific changes in the three bills involved in the *Klinger* case, the court held that these three bills were not effective until July 1, 1972, because they were passed after June 30 and the legislature had not fixed an earlier effective date. As a result, the plaintiffs did not have a justiciable issue which the court acknowledged would have been sufficient grounds for disposing of the case.[41]

The result of this judicial finding has been that both the legislative sponsors and the governor in his amendatory vetoes have found

[41] See Illinois Legislative Council, "Effective Date of Laws," ILC File 8-088 (May 10, 1972), for a more comprehensive discussion of effective dates.

it expedient to insert a section in legislation specifically providing for an effective date. In the spring of 1973 the General Assembly enacted legislation designed to clarify what constitutes "final action." That law (P.A. 78-85) provides that "a bill is 'passed' at the time of its final legislative action prior to presentation to the Governor pursuant to paragraph (a) of Section 9 of Article IV."

4

The Committee System

The basic job of the standing committee is to screen the large volume of bills that floods each legislative session to eliminate those which are defective, unnecessary, or unwise. To allow each committee to perform this task successfully, the scope of its responsibility is limited to a specific subject area that is relatively homogeneous, such as education, human resources, local government, and so on. In working within its jurisdiction, each standing committee can rely principally upon two resources — the experience of its members and a professional staff. A committee operating with a generous supply of these resources, plus the time to utilize them, can give the rest of the legislature the means to make intelligent, reasonable judgments on the legislation that reaches the floor. Standing committees can also reach beyond the screening and reviewing function and play a creative role in the legislative process by investigating problem areas that develop within their jurisdictions and suggesting solutions. Yet the mere presence of all the proper ingredients does not guarantee that the committee system will perform its textbook role.

The existence of a strong committee system can cause a disproportionate reliance upon decisions made in committee. If the power of the committee system becomes excessive, or if the composition of the committees does not reflect that of the body as a whole, then the legislative process can be blocked by a minority, and the representative character of the legislature is severely distorted. On the other hand, if the committee system lacks authority and appropriate resources, then legislative decision making becomes a haphazard guessing game, and individual members are encouraged to rely upon sources outside the immediate control of the legislature for information and advice. These two extremes can be found in Congress and in the Illinois General Assembly. Congressional committees are well financed and well staffed, and the basic seniority system under which they operate insures the longevity of the committee membership. In short, they are equipped with all the facilities that are supposed to result in enlightened public policy, yet the rules and customs of Congress grant committees the power to dominate the legislative process, even against the wishes of a legislative majority. In the Illinois General Assembly standing committees, until recent years, had been denied the resources necessary to play a useful supporting role, and by tradition had been isolated from initiative and responsibility. Somewhere between these two extremes lies the proper environment for the effective utilization of a committee system.

The congressional committee operates independently of the legislative party and its leadership. It is the focal point of the national legislative process, and its influence may be critical to the success or failure of legislation. Congressional committee power gravitates around the chairman, who is usually chosen on the basis of seniority. He is responsible for scheduling hearings and deciding which bills are to be called and when. The choice of committee majority staff is largely his prerogative. He also creates subcommittees, assigns their membership, and decides which proposals they will consider. He acts as floor manager of bills approved by the committee or chooses someone else to do this. By the time a bill reaches the floor it bears the indelible imprint of the committee system.[1]

In the Illinois General Assembly, on the other hand, committee consideration is only one of several equally significant stages in the legislative process. Agreement and compromise frequently occur before or after committee consideration. In both houses staff is hired and assigned to committees (usually after consultation with the individual chairman) by the leadership of each party. The

---

[1] Several of the better studies on congressional committees include: Richard F. Fenno, Jr., *The Power of the Purse — Appropriation Policies in Congress* (Boston: Little, Brown, 1966), and *Congressmen in Committees* (Boston: Little, Brown, 1973); John F. Manley, *The Politics of Finance — The House Committee on Ways and Means* (Boston: Little, Brown, 1970); and "Changing Congress: The Committee System," *The Annals* 411 (January 1974).

scheduling of legislation, as indicated in the previous chapter, is heavily influenced by the desires of individual sponsors. A bill generally will not be posted for hearing if the sponsor indicates he is not ready for it to be heard. Within the limits of the respective tabling rules in each house, committee chairmen do control when individual bills are to be considered. They also have a considerable impact on the action the committee ultimately takes once it has heard a bill. The members of the majority party in either house will generally support the wishes of the committee chairman on most bills. Committee chairmen are, however, considerably more responsive to direction from their party leadership than are congressional committee chairmen. In Congress a chairman can pigeonhole bills indefinitely without hearings or any other explanation, but a committee chairman in the Illinois General Assembly must see that each bill assigned to his or her committee is at least given a hearing. Many noncontroversial bills will come out of committee without amendments, but that does not mean that the committee system cannot be used either to carefully examine and rewrite important legislation or to bottle-up more controversial bills.

The Illinois committee system has encountered a number of obstacles in attempting to become a creative legislative force. In the first place, until recently standing committees of the General Assembly met only during regular sessions of the legislature. In the full six-month session held during the odd year, the committees were hard pressed to review the legislation introduced. In most cases any investigatory or oversight work was delegated to special temporary committees or held for interim commissions. Secondly, Illinois committees were inadequately staffed and were further hampered by an instability of membership. One of the benefits an effective committee operation can bring to the legislative process is the expertise that is largely dependent upon experience. However, committee chairmen and committee membership can change significantly from session to session, limiting the possible accumulated experience of the committee. Finally, legislators simply do not expect the committee to be much of an impediment in the route to final passage. If a disagreement develops in committee, it is not unusual for the bill to be passed out anyway with the understanding that the disputants will settle their differences elsewhere. Thus, agreements may be hammered out on the floor of the House or the Senate, in leadership offices, in the governor's office, or even in the basement coffee shop, rather than in the committee room.[2]

An earlier publication on the Illinois legislature noted that, "As an independent determinant of the fate of legislative proposals, the standing committee is of scant importance."[3] This situation is changing, particularly with respect to the appropriations process. The changing committee role is discussed in greater detail at the end of this chapter.

STRUCTURE AND OPERATION

The structure and operation of the committee system in the Illinois General Assembly is prescribed by the rules of each house, and minor variations may occur from session to session with the adoption of new rules. Generally, the rules specify the number and size of committees, their titles, and the procedures for bill referrals and committee recommendations. There are two general types of standing committees — the legislative committees, that review legislation and make recommendations to their respective chambers, and the service committees, that are concerned with the operation and management of each house.

Under the rules adopted in 1975 there were twenty-two legislative committees in the House, including two appropriations and two judiciary committees. The speaker determined both the size and the membership of each committee, which by rule could not exceed thirty-five members. The leaders of both parties were *ex officio* nonvoting members of each committee. House members other than party leaders could serve on no more than four standing committees.

The 1975 Senate rules provided for a Committee on Commit-

[2] The location of these "bargaining sessions" is not always confined to the capitol complex.

[3] Gilbert Y. Steiner and Samuel K. Gove, *Legislative Politics in Illinois* (Urbana: University of Illinois Press, 1960), p. 82. Within this context, it is interesting to note that the occasional efforts made on the floor to nonconcur with unfavorable committee recommendations are often met with pleas to honor the sanctity of committee decisions. The committee has heard witnesses from both sides, considered the subject extensively, and, thus, its decision should be honored, or so the argument runs. This argument is heard only on occasion because most bills move through committee with little or no trouble, and it is never used to justify the passage of bills, only to uphold unfavorable committee recommendations.

tees to appoint the members of fifteen enumerated standing committees, plus one service committee. Senate rules were silent on committee size and the number of committees on which an individual senator could serve. Nevertheless, after all assignments were made, no committee had more than twenty members, and each senator served on at least two committees and, in most cases, on no more than four. One member of the minority leadership served on six committees. The party membership of committees in the House has tended to closely reflect the partisan division in that chamber, while in the Senate this has not always been the case.

The differences in committee procedures between the two houses generally reflect the difference in size between the two chambers. A comment made by one member of the House is illustrative: "When you have a bill before a House committee, it is generally going to take longer than having the same bill before a Senate committee simply because you have twice as many members on committees in the House as you do in the Senate." Perhaps as a consequence the House rules are more detailed and inclusive than those of the Senate, where smaller numbers prevail and where the membership is more stable and continuous. In practice, however, with the possible exception of the formal use of an interim study calendar in the House, there are no significant differences in the basic operation of the committees in each house.

Committee jurisdictions are not specified by the rules. Instead they are inferred from the title of each committee. Usually, the domain of each standing committee is sufficiently clear-cut to forestall conflicts over jurisdiction. Any conflicts are settled by the majority party leadership in each chamber through its control of the Committee on Assignment of Bills.

Assignments

The membership of each standing committee is determined immediately after the opening of every regular session of the General Assembly. The assignment process is one of the functions performed by the two political parties, and it occurs shortly after the leadership of each house is formally elected. There are no formal criteria that prescribe how committee assignments are made, and the process is primarily dependent upon the preferences of individual members.

If a conflict should arise, however, the wishes of veteran legislators are likely to prevail over those of less experienced members. If there has been a leadership contest, those who backed the winner will fare better than those who did not. The assignment process is described by a long-time House member:

> There's a paper passed to all of the members of the House and they list their committee preferences on the paper in order — one, two, three, four, five — and they turn that paper in to their respective leaders. Then there's a great thrashing around and working out of assignments. One time I remember when we did this in the speaker's office. We had a great big board listing all the committees and we had little hand slips with each member's name on it. We tried to match the slip with his choice, and put him on that committee. There is some degree of flexibility here, but by and large the committee assignments are made or attempted to be made on the basis of each member's choice.

Formal responsibility for committee assignments rests with the speaker of the House and the Committee on Committees in the Senate. In addition to being the presiding officer of the House, the speaker is the leader of his legislative party. He makes committee assignments in consultation with his floor leaders and the leadership of the minority party and he also designates the chairmen and vice-chairmen. In making committee appointments from the minority party, it is customary for him to honor the wishes of the minority leader. Chairmanships and vice-chairmanships, however, usually accrue to majority party members, and their selection is largely a matter of internal party concern, although there have been rare exceptions in the past. By rule no member of the House may serve as chairman or vice-chairman of more than one committee.

In the Senate the rules specify that a Committee on Committees, consisting of ten senators, shall select the membership of each standing committee, subject to the approval of the Senate. There is no provision in the Senate rules for the selection of the chairman of the Committee on Committees or the chairmen of standing committees. By custom, committee assignments and committee chairmanships are now largely the prerogative of the president. In general he follows the same practices that prevail in the House.

It is not unusual for a legislator serving his first term to find all of his preferences for committee assignments fulfilled. In the event that a freshman legislator is not appointed to a desired committee in his first term, it is quite likely he will be appointed to that committee in the next regular session (assuming he is reelected) if he so desires. Rarely are new members selected as committee chairmen, although they may occasionally be chosen as vice-chairmen in a year in which there is a large turnover of members.

The membership on any standing committee in either house is likely to change significantly each session. Some indication of the degree of this change is presented in Table 2, which illustrates the

TABLE 2. MEMBERSHIP TURNOVER IN SELECTED HOUSE COMMITTEES, 1961-75

Committee	Percentage of New Committee Members								
	1961	1963	1965[a]	1967[a]	1969	1971	1973	1975	Average
Appropriations	30.8	41.0	60.0	88.9	46.3	41.7	55.2	68.0[b]	54.0
Education	30.6	38.9	48.1	66.7	63.3	48.1	52.4[b]	44.7[b]	49.1
Executive	43.6	59.0	63.3	88.9	50.0	62.5	58.3	41.7	58.4
Judiciary	25.0	35.0	64.7	55.6	42.8	58.6	58.3[b]	38.9[b]	47.4
Local Government	36.1	27.0	74.1	81.5	46.3	69.7	50.0[b]	61.3[b]	55.8
Average	33.2	40.2	62.0	76.3	49.7	56.1	54.8	50.9	52.9
Percentage of new House members	15.2	17.5	40.7	31.1	25.0	16.9	30.5	20.9	24.7

NOTE: The figures represent percentages of the committee membership who had *not* served on the committee in the previous session.

[a] The rate of turnover is unusually high for the 1965 and 1967 sessions because of the at-large election of House members in 1964. Many of the new members elected in 1964 served only during the 1965 session.

[b] Includes membership on both committees on that subject.

experience over a period of eight biennia of five House committees that customarily handle over half of the legislation referred to committee. The high turnover rate among committee members reflects the absence of seniority as the prime determinant in the selection of committee chairmen, and, to a lesser extent, the influx of new members each session. The party division within each committee reflects the division within either chamber. For example, in the

1973-74 biennium, when the Republicans were in control, the membership of the House Elementary and Secondary Education Committee consisted of thirteen Republicans and eleven Democrats. In the 1975-76 biennium, with a Democratic majority in the chamber, that committee was composed of fourteen Democrats and ten Republicans.

A seniority system demands long and faithful committee service before a member can achieve a position of influence. The ultimate prize — the committee chairmanship — goes to the member of the majority party with the longest service on the committee. In Congress, where the seniority system is well entrenched, the committee chairman monopolizes the considerable powers of his committee, and his job is worth the long wait necessary. Defenders of the seniority system argue that it encourages a stable committee membership and stimulates the accumulated experience and wisdom that allow the committee to be an effective part of the legislative process. Critics, on the other hand, argue that a system which requires only patience and a friendly constituency for success simply rewards mediocrity.

In the Illinois General Assembly the selection of committee chairmen rarely depends upon length of committee service. In fact, in 1971 the chairmen of three of the five committees that were examined had not served on their committees during the previous biennium. Looking at these same five committees, this occurred again in 1973 in two cases and in 1975 in three cases. Legislators do not have to work their way up slowly into a position of influence on a committee. The absence of a seniority system removes a major incentive for a system of stable and continuous committee service.

The influx of new members each session helps to account for a small portion of the high rate of change in committee membership. But as Table 2 clearly indicates, the percentage of new members on each of these five House committees far exceeds the percentage of new House members for each of the seven sessions listed. It is apparent that members of the House change committee assignments frequently from session to session.

Frequent changes in committee assignment occur despite the conviction expressed by many legislators that the development of expertise in specific areas of public policy is extremely helpful in becoming a successful legislator. The following comment by one freshman House member is typical: "Before his first session begins, every legislator should choose a field that interests him and try to become a specialist in that field. Over several sessions, if he acquires expertise in some area, he will be considered the 'spokesman' or 'authority' for the General Assembly whenever bills concerning that particular subject are considered. This is one way of gaining respect and position in the legislature, as well as newspaper publicity. Choosing a specialty is therefore important when trying for committee assignments." Apparently this philosophy has not stimulated lengthy committee service in the House, although it does operate to some degree in the Senate.

Referral of Bills

After each bill is introduced, it is either referred to the Rules Committee or sent to a substantive committee by the Committee on the Assignment of Bills in either house. Most of these decisions are routine and generate little controversy. Since committee jurisdictions can be vague, however, referral can be an arbitrary process.

The chairman of the Committee on the Assignment of Bills usually assigns each bill to committee on the day of its introduction or upon its release by the Rules Committee. The action of the Committee on the Assignment of Bills is reported by the chairman during each daily session when the order of business calls for reports from standing committees. The reports are journalized like any other committee report.[4]

The schedules of the appropriations committees, and of the revenue committees as well, are dependent upon the governor, since

[4] The *Legislative Synopsis and Digest,* published weekly by the Legislative Reference Bureau, also lists action taken on each bill, including committee referrals. This is the handiest source available for determining the progress of individual bills. Legislative Information Systems provides each member with a weekly computer printout of the progress of his or her bills. There are also terminals in various locations which can display information on current bill status and committee action. For those away from the capitol building who desire to follow legislative activity, a private service, the State Capitol Information Service, makes available by subscription a daily summary of all actions taken on bills. The Illinois Manufacturers' Association also publishes a daily legislative report called the "pink sheet" which is widely used.

the great bulk of all fiscal legislation is not introduced until the executive budget is submitted. A bill signed into law by the governor in 1970 changed the statutory date for submission of the budget from April 1 to March 1.[5] A 1973 law requires that all bills implementing this budget be introduced no later than the first Friday in April. These changes have helped somewhat to spread the legislative workload more evenly over the last several months of the session.

Workloads

The number of bills introduced into each successive session of the General Assembly has continued to grow with remarkable persistence with the exception of the 1973-74 biennium when, because of the constitutional change mentioned earlier, the many companion bills which formerly had to be introduced along with one or two important substantive bills were no longer needed.[6] Table 3 shows this change as well as two other basic characteristics of the Illinois committee workload. In each session until 1973 substantial numbers of bills were not considered by a standing committee in either house. The third and fourth columns show the percentages of bills considered in each house that were referred to committee. (A more detailed discussion of the process of advancing bills without reference to committee is presented below.) The last two columns show that prior to 1971 about 80 percent of all the bills referred to committee were reported favorably.

Advancement without Reference to Committee

A sponsor of a bill may desire to expedite passage either because he expects little opposition or because the bill's urgency warrants

---

[5] The Commission on the Organization of the General Assembly recommended that the statutory date be advanced to February 1. A bill implementing this recommendation was passed by the 1969-70 General Assembly but vetoed by the governor.

[6] The Illinois Legislative Council reported that formerly nearly 25 percent of all bills introduced supplemented other bills. These "companion" bills did not in themselves deal with distinct questions of public policy but were integral parts of the "key" bill they accompanied. Once a decision was made on the key bill in a series then the disposition of the companion bills was also determined. Now, these can generally all be combined into one bill.

TABLE 3. COMMITTEE WORKLOADS, REGULAR SESSIONS, 1961-75

	Bills Considered[a]		Bills Referred to Committee[b]		Bills Reported Favorably[c]	
	House	Senate	House	Senate	House	Senate
1975	3,790	2,865	3,689(97%)	2,787(97%)	2,255(61%)	1,672(60%)
1973	2,840	2,261	2,820(99%)	2,169(96%)	1,903(67%)	1,468(68%)
1971	4,579	3,735	4,114(90%)	2,997(80%)	2,909(71%)	1,852(62%)
1969	3,798	3,130	3,622(96%)	2,809(90%)	3,005(83%)	2,440(87%)
1967	3,821	3,511	3,055(80%)	2,765(79%)	2,585(85%)	2,331(84%)
1965	3,328	2,958	2,416(73%)	1,872(63%)	2,028(84%)	1,579(84%)
1963	2,540	2,243	2,054(81%)	1,699(76%)	1,554(76%)	1,338(79%)
1961	2,354	2,076	1,886(80%)	1,358(65%)	1,498(79%)	1,107(82%)

SOURCE: Illinois Legislative Council, "Final Status of Bills" (1961-69). Illinois, Senate, *Journal* (1971) III:4881-5194; House, *Journal* (1971) IV:7443-819. Legislative Information Systems (1973-75).

[a] Includes bills introduced and bills received from the second chamber.

[b] Percentage of all bills considered.

[c] Percentage of all bills referred to committee. Beginning in 1969 some bills which were not reported during the odd-numbered year were ultimately passed during the following year. These bills are not included here.

quick action. Immediately after introduction of a bill or receipt of a message informing the other house of a bill's passage by its house of origin, and after the first reading of that bill, the sponsor may ask for and obtain unanimous consent to have the bill ordered to second reading without referring it to committee. While the Senate rules are silent on the subject, this can be accomplished without controversy only if the chairman of the committee to which it would probably have been assigned agrees to waive committee consideration. Otherwise a roll call is likely to be required, and the wishes of the majority of senators present will prevail. House rules not only require a roll call vote for this procedure to be used, but they require an affirmative vote of three-fifths of the members elected (107) for a bill to bypass committee. The impact of this recent change is reflected in Table 4.

Table 4 shows that since 1973 only 1 or 2 percent of all bills introduced are being advanced without reference to committee in the house of origin. In previous years this figure reached as high as 13 percent. Once a bill reaches the second chamber, its chances of bypassing committee are somewhat better, but still very limited.

TABLE 4. BILLS ADVANCED WITHOUT REFERENCE, 1961-75

Regular Sessions	Bills Introduced[a]	Bills Advanced without Reference in Chamber of Origin[b]	Bills Passed in Chamber of Origin	Bills Advanced without Reference in Second Chamber[b]
1975	4,635	114(2%)[c]	2,020	65(3%)[d]
1973	3,315	27(1%)	1,786	85(5%)
1971	5,084	84(2%)	3,230	437(14%)
1969	4,199	91(2%)	2,729	191(7%)
1967	4,268	185(4%)	3,064	372(12%)
1965	3,590	449(13%)	2,696	858(32%)
1963	2,916	283(10%)	1,867	567(30%)
1961	2,680	169(6%)	1,750	776(44%)

SOURCE: Illinois Legislative Council, "Final Status of Bills" (1961-69). Illinois, Senate, *Journal* (1971) III:4881-5194; House, *Journal* (1971) IV:7443-819. Legislative Information Systems (1973-75).
  [a] House and Senate.
  [b] These figures do not include a substantial number of statutory revision bills that simply combined certain sections and deleted obsolete language in the body of statute law, making no substantive changes in the law itself. They were traditionally advanced without reference to committee. Under the new constitution all of these changes can be included in one bill.
  [c] Percentage of all bills introduced.
  [d] Percentage of all bills passed in the chamber of origin.

The chances of passage also increase somewhat. As Table 5 indicates, the house of origin holds the greater danger of failure for legislation.

THE COMMITTEE CHAIRMAN

The committee system has started to gain some strength, and committee chairmen are becoming more important also. Their influence can be seen on the floor of either house when attempts are made to bypass or discharge a committee. Generally neither chamber will go against the desires of the committee chairman affected except on a controversial issue where that chairman has succeeded in keeping a particular piece of legislation in committee. Legislation sponsored by the chairman of the committee from which it is reported seems to have a definite impact on the membership of both chambers, particularly the second house. For example, it is highly unlikely that an appropriation bill sponsored by the chairman of either appropriations committee will meet with any serious resistance. This is also true with legislation that is highly complex and difficult

TABLE 5. BILL PASSAGE BY HOUSE AND SENATE,[a] 1961-75

Regular Sessions	Bills Failing Chamber of Origin[b]		Bills Failing Second Chamber[c]	
	House	Senate	House	Senate
1975	43%	44%	17%	36%
1973	50%	40%	37%	38%
1971	36%	38%	38%	45%
1969	36%	32%	14%	8%
1967	31%	25%	16%	13%
1965	28%	20%	13%	14%
1963	40%	30%	9%	8%
1961	34%	36%	11%	9%

SOURCE: Illinois Legislative Council, "Final Status of Bills" (1961-69). Illinois, Senate, *Journal* (1971) III:4881-5194; House, *Journal* (1971) IV:7443-819. Legislative Information Systems (1973-75).
[a] Only bills introduced and passed during the odd-year regular sessions are considered here. Otherwise bills are considered to have failed.
[b] Percentage of all bills introduced during odd-year regular session.
[c] Percentage of all bills passed by the house of origin.

to understand. Legislation changing the school aid formula which has the imprimatur of the chairman of the Education Committee will fare much better than legislation offered on the same subject by a noncommittee member. Related to this influence is the developing use of committee-sponsored bills in which the chairman generally handles the legislation.

Committee chairmen also enjoy a greater degree of public visibility than do other legislators, particularly among those groups or professions which are most directly affected by legislation which is considered by a particular committee. With the development of a permanent professional staff, the chairman and the minority spokesman are now receiving more resource material on legislation assigned to their committee. Insofar as they are able to direct the staff effort — and "knowledge is power" — committee chairmen are beginning to have an impact on shaping the content of legislation which comes out of their committees. This has resulted in a greater percentage of bills being reported out of committee with committee amendments attached.

Committee chairmen also exercise some power as presiding officers at committee hearings. Although the rules of both houses govern committee procedure as far as they are applicable, committee hearings are usually free-flowing operations in which the chairman exercises a good deal of discretion. The chairman determines the order in which bills will be considered and the time allotted for testimony on each bill. He also rules on procedural questions. However, the chairman usually cannot kill or pigeonhole bills or take any action that will significantly affect the future of a bill.

A chairman can play a positive and occasionally crucial role in committee if he has the support of a majority of the committee membership. With such support, the chairman can dominate a committee hearing; without it, his influence is severely circumscribed.

Hearings and Recommendations

Even though the screening of bills is obviously their primary function during regular sessions of the General Assembly, the standing committees have generally displayed a great reluctance to hinder the passage of legislation. For the vast majority of bills, committee consideration is still limited to one, brief, favorable hearing, although this is changing. Committees are usually inclined to approve legislation if there is no opposition. Frequently committee chairmen will ask if there is any opposition to the bill being considered. If no voice is raised in opposition at this point, the bill will be reported out with a "do pass" recommendation. Some committees are beginning to be more cautious about what bills they allow out onto the floor. Whereas previously all bills on the same subject would usually be voted out to allow the entire body to decide which to pass, the practice of developing one committee bill on a given subject (as is done in Congress) is becoming more popular.

At one time little organized preparation preceded committee hearings. Although copies of statements made by witnesses before a standing committee might have occasionally been distributed at the hearing, seldom, if ever, did committee members have the opportunity to acquire copies prior to the meeting. Consequently, most questions asked by committee members were generated spontaneously rather than being the result of advance homework. Although these conditions are still present to some extent, professional staff assistance is now more universally available to each committee on a partisan basis. Thus, the committee members are often able to develop very rapidly a strong line of questioning from the staff memorandum on each bill that is made available to them prior to the committee meeting.

As noted previously, the great bulk of the legislation referred to committee customarily receives some type of favorable recommendation. Such recommendations have as a result not necessarily assured a bill a favorable reception on the floor, although this too has been changing in some respects. If a committee has begun to develop a reputation for screening the bills assigned to it and not reporting all proposed legislation out onto the floor, the bills which it does report appear to have a better than average chance at passage. Again, this depends on the reputation and influence of the committee and its chairman. Table 6 shows how many bills were referred to each committee in both houses during the 1973 and 1975 sessions, and how many of those bills were favorably reported.

The results of an unfavorable committee report are usually more conclusive than is a "do pass" recommendation, for the legislature has shown a great reluctance to overturn committees on these matters. A bill reported unfavorably is dead unless the sponsor makes a successful motion to nonconcur with the committee recommendation when the bill is reported on the floor. If a motion is made and is supported by a majority of the members elected, the bill will be placed upon the calendar.

As mentioned above, committee amendments are being offered for an increasing number of bills, and most of these are readily adopted by the legislature since they are unlikely to generate controversy. Amendments offered by a standing committee tend to be technical rather than substantive and, if they do effect a substantive change, are usually offered with the consent and blessing of all parties concerned. Committee consideration of most bills is limited to one hearing, and most amendments are worked out in advance. Thus, any controversy is likely to have been settled before the committee considers the bill. In the event that conflict does develop in the committee, the parties to the dispute are customarily encouraged to come to some verbal agreement so that the bill can be reported out of committee and later amended on the floor. There are, again, more and more exceptions to the rule as certain committees become stronger. The appropriation committees in particular have become

TABLE 6. SCREENING OF BILLS BY COMMITTEE, 1973 AND 1975

Committee	Number of Bills Referred		Number of Bills Favorably Reported		Percent Favorable	
	1973	1975	1973	1975	1973	1975
House						
Agriculture and Natural Resources[a]	187	164	131	86	70	52
Appropriations[b]	458	421	329	320	72	76
Banks and Savings and Loans	55	191	32	125	58	65
Cities and Villages	154	199	108	117	70	59
Counties and Townships	185	351	120	201	65	57
Elections	104	157	64	74	62	47
Elementary and Secondary Education	146	216	105	106	72	49
Executive	275	509	177	249	64	49
Higher Education	62	81	43	40	69	49
Human Resources	141	191	105	102	74	53
Insurance	49	79	32	51	65	65
Judiciary I	169	210	108	94	64	45
Judiciary II	150	225	86	112	57	50
Labor and Commerce[c]	55	147	32	97	58	66
Motor Vehicles	132	127	74	64	56	50
Personnel and Pensions[d]	176	217	114	113	65	52
Public Utilities	38	62	19	30	50	48
Revenue	157	232	88	82	56	35
Transportation	126	177	79	110	63	62
Veterans' Affairs, Registration, and Regulation[e]	108	156	57	82	53	53
	2,927	4,112	1,903	2,255	65	55
Senate						
Agriculture, Conservation, and Energy[f]	95	142	69	109	73	77
Appropriations	330	341	258	221	78	65
Education	177	185	137	131	77	71
Elections and Reapportionment	67	92	52	67	78	73
Executive[g]	186	396	94	191	51	48
Finance and Credit Regulations[h]	48	127	22	79	46	62
Insurance and Licensed Activities[i]	88	143	55	95	63	66
Judiciary	290	371	177	125	61	34
Labor and Commerce[j]	44	92	17	52	39	57
Local Government	268	291	196	201	73	69
Pensions, Personnel, and Veterans' Affairs[k]	121	170	75	113	62	66

(Table 6, *continued*)

Committee	Number of Bills Referred		Number of Bills Favorably Reported		Percent Favorable	
	1973	1975	1973	1975	1973	1975
Public Health, Welfare, and Corrections	120	135	79	98	66	73
Revenue	127	156	64	87	50	56
Transportation[l]	213	146	173	103	81	71
	2,174	2,787	1,468	1,672	68	60

NOTE: When a bill is rereferred to a second committee in the same chamber it is counted twice for purposes of this table, once for each committee. As a result, the total number of bills referred to all committees in either chamber may exceed the total number of bills considered in that chamber. In most cases such a bill will be favorably reported out of only one committee. Rules Committee referrals are not reflected in any of these totals.

Committee names and/or jurisdictions do not correspond exactly in every case for the 1973 and the 1975 sessions. These exceptions are noted as follows:

[a] 1975 figures are combined totals for both the Agriculture Committee and the Environment, Energy, and Natural Resources Committee. The 1973 name is used in the table.

[b] 1975 figures are combined totals for both appropriations committees.

[c] Industrial Affairs in 1973.

[d] Veterans Affairs, Personnel, and Pensions in 1973.

[e] Registration and Regulation in 1973.

[f] Agriculture, Conservation and Ecology in 1973.

[g] 1975 figures are combined totals for both the Executive Committee and the Executive Appointments and Administration Committee.

[h] Licensed Activities and Credit Regulations in 1973.

[i] Insurance and Financial Institutions in 1973.

[j] Industry and Labor in 1973.

[k] Pensions and Personnel in 1973.

[l] Transportation and Public Utilities in 1973.

stronger; a majority of these committees' amendments are usually, but not always, upheld on the floor, even on controversial issues.

If a committee holds a bill, perhaps by sending it to a subcommittee, the sponsor may move to discharge the standing committee from further consideration of his bill. Subcommittees — and in the House, the interim study calendar — can be a means of pigeon-holing a bill without actually killing it with a "do not pass" recommendation. Some subcommittees, though, have done a substantial amount of work and reported legislation back to the full committee, usually with some substantive changes.

To discharge a committee, a sponsor must make a motion to that effect on the floor. In the Senate, if a sponsor's motion to discharge a committee is supported by a majority of the Senate's full membership, the committee is obliged to release the bill. In the House of

Representatives, a committee may be relieved of a bill by a motion supported by a majority of the members, provided that notice has been given on the preceding legislative day so that the motion appears on the calendar on the day it is debated.

A bill taken from a committee goes on the calendar or is referred to another committee, depending on the nature of the discharge motion. Each session a number of bills are taken from committees in this way, although the requirement of an affirmative vote equal to that required for passage makes this procedure difficult to use. Generally, unless a bipartisan coalition of noncommittee members has been organized, it is almost impossible to take a bill from committee without the chairman's consent because many members will vote against a discharge motion even if they support the legislation involved.

Records of committee meetings are very incomplete. The rules require that the committee clerk record only the time and place of each meeting, the attendance, the vote on each bill or resolution, and, in the House only, the names and addresses of witnesses. House rules also require that every committee roll call be recorded in the House *Journal* along with the committee's report. After each session the records are sent to the State Archives (a division of the State Library). Committee records do not provide a verbatim transcript or even a limited account of debate or testimony, except in extraordinary circumstances.

COMMITTEE OF THE WHOLE

In addition to the standing committees of each house, the General Assembly relies upon a number of other types of committees to complete the task of lawmaking. While the legislature is in session, the House or the Senate may occasionally convene a Committee of the Whole, consisting of the entire membership of the chamber concerned, to hear testimony on a bill or problem of unusual or widespread interest. A Committee of the Whole meeting allows all members of the House or Senate the opportunity to hear testimony and ask questions from outside witnesses, and in general to conduct a less formal discussion than would be possible in a regular session of either house. Unlike other legislative bodies, the Committee of the Whole takes no formal action on bills considered. A bill may be considered in a Committee of the Whole as well as being heard before a standing committee. In accord with recent practice, consideration by a Committee of the Whole, when it does take place, precedes reference to a standing committee.

Either house may go into Committee of the Whole on a motion to that effect or at a time designated previously by the adoption of a special order. The motion must specify the bill or bills or other business to be considered. In the House, a bill or resolution can be considered in Committee of the Whole only after the regular six-and-one-half day notice requirement has been met. The motion to resolve either house into a Committee of the Whole is usually adopted several days in advance. When the appointed hour arrives, the presiding officer designates another member as chairman; frequently this person will be the chairman of the standing committee that would otherwise hear the bill or will consider the bill later. After the business of the Committee of the Whole is completed, the meeting is ended by a motion to rise and report. The regular presiding officer then returns to his chair, and the chairman of the committee reports for the journal record what progress was made, usually that a "general discussion" was held. In the House, the rules specifically prohibit offering amendments in a Committee of the Whole.

JOINT COMMITTEES AND SPECIAL INVESTIGATING COMMITTEES

Joint committees and special investigating committees are both temporary committees created by resolution to supplement the activities of the standing committees during regular sessions of the General Assembly. Joint committees are made up of members of both the House and Senate and consider areas of particular concern to the legislature. In 1973 Senate Joint Resolution No. 10 established a joint subcommittee of the House and Senate revenue committees, consisting of six members of each committee, to study the property tax and possible ways of reforming it. Over an eighteen-month period it held hearings all over the state and developed, at the very least, a small group of experts on a complex problem that defies simple solutions. The success of this joint subcommittee, whose membership corresponded to that of the two standing committees on revenue, may lead to a greater use of this approach for in-depth studies of long-term problems.[7]

The General Assembly makes use of its investigatory power by means of special committees which are directed by resolution to investigate specific problems and recommend appropriate solutions to the legislature. Senate Resolution No. 49 adopted by the regular session of the 1971-72 General Assembly is typical. Senate Resolution No. 49 created a subcommittee of the Senate Committee on Local Government to investigate and consider charges concerning abuses in the administration of the Chicago Dwellings Association. A special investigating committee may be the creature of only one house or it may be a joint committee with both houses represented. More often, one or both houses will pass a resolution instructing the Legislative Investigating Commission to look into a given problem and report back to the legislature.

Conference Committees

Conference committees, as discussed in the previous chapter, are appointed to resolve differences between House and Senate on the final form of legislation. Disagreement between the houses has sometimes been limited to only a dozen or so controversial bills during the course of a session, but other times nearly all major bills, particularly appropriation bills, have ended up in conference. In recent years there is no question but that the use of conference committees (and second conference committees — see below) has been increasing. On those occasions when the two houses are still at odds after exchanging formal messages and consulting informally, a conference committee is appointed by the speaker of the House and the Committee on Committees in the Senate to work out a mutually acceptable solution. The conference committee is really a joint meeting of two committees — one from each house — composed usually of five members each. The committee exists only to consider a single

[7] On October 4 and 7, 1974, the *Champaign-Urbana Courier* commented favorably on the serious attention this Senate-House panel was giving to the whole question of the Illinois property tax system. The serious use of joint committees or subcommittees is a marked departure from the former dependence on legislative commissions.

bill and disbands after making its report to both chambers. No witnesses are heard and meetings, while open to the public, are often hard to find as they can occur any place ten or fewer people can assemble. Many conference committees never even meet in a formal sense. One house or the other will back down, or both will remain firm in their positions, and a simple report will be circulated by staff among the committee members for their signatures. As one recent freshman member of the Senate remarked, "In the two years I've been here, I've been appointed to nine and I've yet to attend a meeting."[8]

The conference is limited to the area of disagreement, and the conferees are likely to agree on a report providing for concessions on the part of both houses. Conference reports on appropriation bills must relate directly to "matters of difference" that have been specifically referred to the conference committee. This restriction is intended to prevent surprises in appropriation bills. Conference reports are signed in duplicate by those conferees who concur and are then sent to each house. Technically, the disagreeing house must receive its copy first. The rules require that the report should be agreed to by a majority of the delegation from each house before submission to each chamber. In the event that a conference committee fails to come to an agreement and formally reports the deadlock, a second committee may be appointed. If after two conferences the houses fail to agree on a common text of a bill, then it is lost.

INTERIM AND CONTINUING COMMISSIONS

Between regular sessions of the General Assembly, interim commissions used to be organized to supplement the narrow bill-screening focus of the standing committees by engaging in broad fact-finding investigations. During the past several years, with the legislature now sitting as a continuous body, the standing committees have started to assume a greater portion of this work. Legislative leaders from both parties have cooperated in insisting that an extraordinary reason exist before any new commissions are created. Also, legislation has been introduced periodically which would severely limit

[8] Richard H. Icen, "Committees — Bane of the Legislature," *Champaign-Urbana Courier,* July 29, 1974.

the number of continuing commissions by eliminating and consolidating many of the existing commissions.

Each enabling statute creating an interim commission directs it to explore a specific problem area and report back to the legislature, usually at the beginning of the next General Assembly, with specific recommendations.[9] As a means of controlling the number of commission bills which pass each year, the General Assembly has begun using an omnibus appropriation bill for funding those commissions which were "agreed" on. As a result, commission proposals have been acted on either in the appropriation committees or at the amendment stage on the floor. This has also served to reduce the amount of time which is spent debating and voting on each individual commission request for five, ten, or even twenty thousand dollars.[10]

In addition to temporary study commissions the General Assembly is responsible for the creation of a large number of continuing, permanent commissions which perform a variety of functions. A number of continuing commissions, with both legislative and public members, have been created to act in advisory capacities to certain agencies within the executive branch and to coordinate their activities with the legislative branch of state government. Among the advisory commissions active during recent biennia have been the Toll Road Advisory Committee, which meets with the Illinois State Toll Highway Commission to advise it on matters relating to the administration of the toll highway system; the Judicial Advisory Council, which is charged with reviewing and mediating the needs

[9] Bills creating interim study commissions, unlike resolutions creating temporary investigating committees, are subject to approval by the governor, which has not always been forthcoming. Both interim study commissions and temporary investigating committees have at their command the power to subpoena witnesses and records pertinent to their investigations. Because these are interim bodies, the enabling acts usually provide for their automatic repeal within two years.

[10] An analysis of legislative actions required to pass the fiscal year 1974 budget compiled by the majority staff director of the House Appropriations Committee revealed that while the appropriation bills for the legislative and judicial branches as well as for several minor agencies accounted for only 1.2 percent of the total dollars appropriated, they represented 46 percent of the budget bill workload, 47 percent of the roll calls required to pass the state budget, and 37 percent of the total legislative actions required to pass the state budget (memorandum of January 21, 1974, from Donald S. Glickman to Rep. James R. Washburn, Chairman, House Committee on Appropriations).

and requests of all levels of the state's judicial system; the Council on Aging, which is an advisory group for the Department of Aging on problems facing the state's senior citizens; and the Legislative Advisory Committee on Public Aid, which advises the Department of Public Aid on matters relating to the administration of public assistance programs. Several continuing commissions represent the state of Illinois on a rapidly expanding number of interstate commissions, such as the Education Commission of the States and the Multistate Tax Commission. In recent years, according to the Illinois Legislative Council, there have usually been about twenty advisory committees and special committees of interstate compacts in existence.

The greatest number of continuing commissions are study groups concerned with particular problem areas which are required to report back to each regular session of the General Assembly. A partial listing should indicate some of the major areas of legislative concern: the Commission on Children, the School Problems Commission, the Cities and Villages Municipal Problems Commission, the County Problems Commission, the Dangerous Drugs Commission, the Economic Development Commission, the Election Laws Commission, the Energy Resources Commission, the Insurance Laws Study Commission, the Labor Laws Study Commission, the Mental Health and Developmentally Disabled Commission, the Motor Vehicle Laws Commission, the Pension Laws Commission, the Spanish Speaking Peoples Study Commission, the Commission on the Status of Women, the Urban Education Commission, and the Commission to Visit and Examine State Institutions. Permanent study commissions are expressions of a continuing legislative concern with certain areas of public policy, and their use has been increasing steadily over the past few years, despite concern for their undue proliferation. In 1961 there were twenty-six continuing commissions (including six advisory commissions and fifteen interim commissions). Since that time the number has grown to approximately sixty (including almost twenty advisory commissions). Included in this total are the various commissions concerned in some way with housekeeping aspects of legislative activity such as the Senate Operations Commission and the Board of Trustees of the General Assembly Retirement System.

Also included in the above total are eight permanent service agencies to the General Assembly. These (and the years in which they were established) are the Legislative Reference Bureau (1913), the Legislative Council (1937), the Commission on Intergovernmental Cooperation (1937), the Legislative Audit Commission (1957), the Legislative Space Needs Commission (1967), the Illinois Legislative Investigating Commission (1971), the Illinois Economic and Fiscal Commission (1972), and Legislative Information Systems (1975).

A Changing Committee Role

In its report to the 1967-68 General Assembly, the Commission on the Organization of the General Assembly (COOGA) concluded that standing committees were not performing their most important function — screening bills to eliminate defective or unnecessary legislation. This is not a new complaint. As the speaker of the House observed about twenty years ago, "I think we would be able to conduct more business more efficiently if the committees would find a bad bill bad and say so at the committee level." The commission suggested that the bill-screening process was inadequate for the following reasons:

> Committees rarely have enough information to permit a confident judgment of death to be entered against a bill; committees may feel reassured that several difficult hurdles remain to be surmounted before a bill that comes out of committee becomes law . . . ; in the absence of organized opposition, there is no mechanism for inquiring into a bill and therefore no reason to do other than pass it through the committee; and committees are rarely willing to be discriminating enough to instill confidence in the membership or in informed observers that the committee function is being properly exercised in Illinois.[11]

To bolster the ability of committees to function as effective bill-screening devices, the commission suggested professional committee staffing, streamlined committee jurisdictions, mandatory committee

[11] Illinois, General Assembly, Commission on the Organization of the General Assembly, *Improving the State Legislature* (Urbana: University of Illinois Press, 1967), p. 52.

referral for all bills introduced, and the joint operation between regular sessions of the legislature of House and Senate committees sharing the same jurisdiction. In each biennium since the COOGA report was issued in 1967, the General Assembly has taken additional steps to improve committee procedures and thereby expand committee influence. Throughout this chapter we have pointed to changes which have been made to bolster the effectiveness and influence of committees and committee chairmen. Committee referral has become almost mandatory, particularly in the House. Committee jurisdictions have been streamlined, although not as severely as recommended in the COOGA report, with comparable committees sharing the same jurisdiction in each house. About one-third of the fifteen Senate committees have, however, two, and in one case three, comparable committees in the House. The use of joint committees and subcommittees as study groups between sessions has also begun to develop. In addition a number of significant procedural changes have been effected in the House rules, such as the complete elimination of voting by proxy and the requirement that a committee take final action on a bill within forty-five days after receiving it. Both of these changes were discussed earlier.

Perhaps the most significant development has been the provision for permanent professional committee staffing. Prior to 1967 the only such staff assistance available to the legislature came through the legislative intern program instituted in 1961. The intern program helped to fill the "staff gap" to some extent, but the need for full-time professional staff assistance remained. As the COOGA commission suggested, one of the primary requisites for an effective committee operation is the availability of staff assistance. While not every committee is yet fully staffed with its own personnel, both political parties in both houses now have enough assistance that the committees are able to do a better job of seriously scrutinizing the merits of each bill. The Appropriations Committee of each house has benefited the most from this change as the legislature has moved rapidly toward gaining a better understanding of the state's budget and thereby increasing its ability to have a genuine impact upon the appropriations process. New department directors have learned that they must do more than convince the Bureau of the Budget and the governor of the necessity of their requests. The state budget bills signed into law in July may now include some significant differences from what the governor proposes in March.

In addition to professional staff assistance, committees of the General Assembly seem to be taking further steps toward a more aggressive role in the legislative process. The move toward annual legislative sessions has provided the standing committees of the legislature with an opportunity to expand their activities throughout the two-year life of each session. The appropriations process serves again as a good illustration.

In its 1967 report the COOGA commission made the following observations about what happened to an appropriation bill in the appropriations committees:

> Legislative participation in the appropriations process appears to have had just one purpose: to pass appropriation bills.
>
> It seems apparent, then, that the appropriations committees act as little more than way stations that must be visited by each bill as it proceeds along the well-marked route which leads to a final floor vote.[12]

Using 1963 data, the commission noted that 80.3 percent of all bills referred to the appropriations committees that year were reported out with no amendments and a "do pass" recommendation; 9.7 percent were amended in committee; 1.6 percent were formally reported out with a "do not pass" recommendation; 2.4 percent were either tabled or remained in committee at the end of the session; and 5.9 percent were removed from committee consideration by a vote of the respective house.

Ten years later the majority staff of the House Appropriations Committee found that the number of bills referred to the two appropriations committees increased from 370 in 1963 to 765 in 1973 — an increase of more than 100 percent. The percentage of bills coming out of these committees with no amendments and a "do pass" recommendation dropped from 80.3 percent in 1963 to 44.2 percent in 1973. The percentage of bills which were amended in committee increased from 9.7 percent in 1963 to 31.6 percent in 1973. In absolute numbers "do pass as amended" bills increased from 36 in 1963 to 242 in 1973, a seven-fold increase. The over-

[12] *Ibid.,* pp. 101, 108.

whelming majority of amendments in 1973 were committee amendments, not member-sponsored amendments. The two committees
increased their "do not pass" recommendations from 1.6 percent
of the bills considered in 1963 to 4.7 percent in 1973. Bills that
were either tabled or remained in committee increased from 2.4 percent in 1963 to 14.1 percent in 1973. When the last two categories
are considered together (which gives a better indicator of negative
committee action), it can be seen that unfavorable committee actions
increased from 4.0 percent in 1963 to 18.8 percent in 1973. The
1963 and 1973 percentages on bills discharged from committee are
almost identical, dipping only slightly from 5.9 percent in 1963 to
5.4 percent in 1973. In both years most of the bills in this latter
category were taken from the Senate Appropriations Committee.[13]

Increasing activity on the part of these and other standing committees may signify a new, positive attitude among members of the
General Assembly toward renovation of the traditional committee
system. Some substantive committees have been holding more bills
in committee, as well as amending more of the bills they receive.
Once individual committees begin to develop reputations for reporting only those bills which will win the approval of a majority
of the entire membership on the floor, there will be tangible evidence
that a viable, effective committee system is indeed evolving.[14]

[13] Memorandum of August 1, 1973, by Donald S. Glickman, to Speaker
W. Robert Blair, "The House Appropriations Committee: A Comparison of
Committee Actions for 1963 and 1973."
[14] For a comparative analysis of how legislative committees operate in other
states, as well as in Illinois, see Alan Rosenthal, *Legislative Performance in the
States* (New York: Free Press, 1974).

5

Legislative Service: Privileges, Problems, and Pressures

Perhaps the most obvious characteristic of lawmaking in Illinois is that comparatively few people pursue it full time, although the ranks of those who do are growing. Most legislators are not in a position to devote all of their time and energy to the task of making laws and many would argue that full-time service is unnecessary. The concept of the part-time legislator is a well-established American political tradition. In the early days of the Republic, members of the state and national legislatures could easily meet the responsibilities of office by taking a few weeks off each winter from their law practices, their farms, or their factories to carry on the business of government. That schedule has persisted in various forms to this day.

Through the 1920s, sessions of Congress began in December and ended before summer. There was little doubt that membership in Congress was a part-time pursuit. Depression and war disrupted the tranquility of Washington, D.C., and changed a sleepy southern town to a place where the nation's government is big business. In 1946 Congress initiated a pension plan for its members, a recognition that service in Congress is a career in itself. At the same time Congress set July 31 as the deadline for adjournment. That deadline has never been met.

In Illinois a number of elements contributed to the maintenance of a part-time legislature until the late 1960s. In the first place, the General Assembly formerly enjoyed an active life span of only six months each biennium. With the important exception of the extended sessions in the late 1960s, the basic demand on each legislator's time was limited to the regular session and to periodic commission meetings between sessions. On rare occasions the governor called a special session. For the most part, however, the bulk of each member's legislative activity took place when the General Assembly was actually in session, and even then he had a generous amount of time to devote to other pursuits. The regular legislative sessions have begun as recently as 1973 and 1975 with a leisurely pace in January, which increased with each succeeding month, and ended with a dramatic surge in late June and on into July. The same general pattern has developed for sessions in even-numbered years, although there have been more interruptions because of primary elections. Fall sessions of approximately six weeks' duration have been, however, a recent development. During the regular spring session, activity usually has been limited to a Monday to Thursday or Tuesday to Friday sequence until the last weeks. In addition, all legislators spend time serving their districts when they are at home, engaging in political chores, and running for office every two or four years. The time spent outside the legislative arena is usually quite significant.

There is a definite trend toward longer legislative sessions, confirmed by the recent extended and special sessions. In 1955 both the House and the Senate were in session for only 67 days, while in 1965 this rose to 93 days in the House and 101 days in the Senate. In the 1975 session of the Seventy-ninth General Assembly, the House met for 114 days, the Senate for 96. As the amount of work facing the legislature increases, this trend can be expected to continue.

LEGISLATORS AND THEIR OFFICES

In addition to the temporal element, two other factors have stimulated the continuation of part-time legislators. Although legislators' salaries in Illinois have been consistently higher than in most other states, they have not usually been sufficient to allow members to abandon private sources of income.[1] The obvious insecurity of political life has been another prime factor encouraging legislators to continue their interests in private business or professional life.[2] Until recently there was little reason to expect lawmaking to be the exclusive or dominant concern in a legislator's life, and service in Springfield was viewed by most members as a "legislative interlude."

A former presiding officer of the Illinois Senate, in reviewing his nearly two decades of service in the General Assembly, remarked, "Eventually we must have full-time legislators; it is almost that now. So long as legislators view the assembly as a necessary interruption of their regular duties as lawyers, teachers, or whatever, the yearning to go home or get the meeting over with will dominate much assembly activity."[3]

A decade ago, the California legislature faced most of the problems that have been frustrating Illinois legislators in recent years: low pay, poor facilities, inadequate staff, and sessions that had mushroomed from brief, biennial events in the late 1940s to a ten-and-one-half month marathon in 1965. As in Illinois today, good men — weary of impossible workloads, endless chores in their dis-

[1] Salaries for legislators in Illinois have risen from the 1895 level of $3,000 per biennium to $3,500 in 1915, $5,000 in 1937, $6,000 in 1947, $10,000 in 1953, $12,000 in 1959, $12,000 annually in 1969, $17,500 annually in 1971, and finally to $20,000 annually in 1975. The four legislative leaders (the speaker of the House, the president of the Senate, and the minority leaders in both houses) receive an additional increment of up to $10,000. Only legislators in California ($21,120) and New York ($23,500) receive higher salaries. The lowest paid state legislators are found in New Hampshire, where the biennial compensation is only $200 (Source: Jane Van Sant, "How Much Are State Legislators Paid?: A Report on Salaries, Allowances and Benefits in the 50 States," *Research Memorandum* 18, Citizens Conference on State Legislatures (September 1975)). See the section that follows on some rewards and costs of legislative service.

[2] This necessary reliance upon outside interests does not mean that the General Assembly is split into occupational blocs. Lawyers are the largest single occupational group and normally constitute about 30 percent of the membership. However, there is little evidence to suggest that lawyers characteristically vote as a bloc. The second largest group is comprised of those who list themselves as full-time legislators. The next largest occupational group consists of real estate and insurance brokers.

[3] In the summer 1974 issue of *State Government*, two members of the Colorado House of Representatives present differing views on the desirability of having full-time legislators. See Charles B. Howe, "The Case for . . . The Professional Legislator," and Michael L. Strang, "The Case for . . . The Citizen Legislator," 47:130-36.

tricts, hurried meetings with constituents, little or no personal staff assistance, increasing time away from their families, and dwindling income from neglected outside jobs — were leaving.

Not too long ago Alan Rosenthal noted that this continues to be the trend in nearly every other state legislature: "It is still hard to attract and then hold the most able men in legislative service. Turnover in state legislatures is high, more than twice as high as in the U.S. Congress. After an average election, perhaps one-third of the members are replaced by newcomers. Nor is it certain that the best members make the legislature their career or stay long enough to make a real difference."[4]

Experience is undoubtedly an important factor in the development of competent legislators, but a number of other factors seem equally significant. The ability of the political system to recruit able prospects, the attractiveness of legislative salaries and working conditions, the presence of professional staff assistance, to name a few, are all important elements in attracting and developing top-grade legislators.

TURNOVER

In recent years the movement of members in and out of the legislative fraternity has fluctuated. An abnormally high number of voluntary retirements made the freshman class of 1973 as large or nearly as large as the classes of such banner years as 1957, 1965, and 1967. In the Senate, the number of newcomers reached record proportions. In line with a continuing trend, more women were elected to the General Assembly in 1974 than in any previous year — three in the Senate and twelve in the House. In 1975, one of these twelve House members became the first female assistant minority leader.

A large preponderance of new members in any legislative body is a source of concern to some observers and participants. Experience, the argument goes, is a precious commodity. Familiarity with the machinery of the legislative process enables the legislator to confront his environment effectively, while a thorough knowledge of existing legislation and past proposals enables him to exercise sound and discriminating judgment on the wisdom of proposed legislation.

[4] Alan Rosenthal, "The Scope of Legislative Reform — An Introduction," in *Strengthening the States*, p. 5.

Underlying this argument over longevity is the fear that the presence of large numbers of new members unfamiliar with the ins and outs of the legislative process will limit major decision making by default to a handful of veteran legislators. Whether or not representative government is distorted by the presence of legislators unfamiliar with the mechanics of the legislative process and the customs and folkways of the legislature is a matter of conjecture. A number of other influences operate in the legislative arena that tend to overshadow the relative inexperience of a few members. The most that can be said is that the effectiveness of the new legislator tends to be diminished by his lack of knowledge of the "rules of the game." This deficiency has been recognized and in some states steps have been taken to remedy the situation. The recent appearance of orientation conferences for new legislators is testimony to this concern.

In terms of accumulated legislative experience, however, the Illinois House of Representatives ranks high among American state legislatures. In 1973, for example, 41 percent of all state legislators in all fifty states were serving their first terms. In the Illinois House an extraordinarily large freshman class was still less than three-fourths of this national average.[5] Over the years cumulative voting has consistently insured a relatively stable House membership. The Illinois Senate also displays a more stable membership than the average of its counterparts in the other forty-nine states. However, there is still a substantial turnover in personnel at each regular session of the General Assembly. Usually about one out of every four House members is serving his first term. In the Senate the ratio averages one out of eight. The amount of turnover in the ten regular sessions held between 1957 and 1975 is listed in Table 7.

The greater legislative experience found among members of the Illinois Senate is a result of the longer four-year Senate term and

[5] In recent years the highest rate of first-term membership in a lower house has been in Louisiana (68 percent), the lowest in Hawaii (16 percent). Among upper houses Iowa has had the highest rate of first-term membership (60 percent). In five states there were no election contests in 1972 and therefore no members serving their apprenticeships the following year. Of the states which had upper house seats up for election in 1972, California had the lowest turnover (15 percent). See *The Book of the States, 1974-75* (Lexington, Ky.: Council of State Governments), p. 69.

TABLE 7. FIRST-TERM MEMBERSHIP, 1957-75

Session	Senate		House	
	Number	Percent[a]	Number	Percent[a]
1975	5	8.5	36	20.3
1973	14	23.7	54	30.5
1971	9	15.5	29	16.4
1969	2[c]	3.4	37	20.9
1967[b]	10	17.2	55	31.1
1965[b]	8	13.8	72	40.7
1963	5	8.6	31	17.5
1961	4	6.9	27	15.2
1959	8	13.8	22	12.4
1957	12	20.6	67	37.8
Average	8	13.9	44	24.7

NOTE: These figures include *only those members serving their first terms in the General Assembly.*
    [a] Percentage of total membership — 59 in the Senate and 177 in the House (prior to 1973 the Senate had 58 members).
    [b] The figures for 1965 and 1967 are somewhat higher than usual due to the large influx of new House members as a result of the 1964 at-large election and subsequent reapportionment of both houses. Reapportionments are also reflected in the large figures for 1957 and 1973.
    [c] In 1966 all 58 senators were elected for four-year terms; only two vacancies occurred in the 1969-70 General Assembly.

frequent intercameral movement from House to Senate.[6] In fact, advancement from House to Senate is an established tradition in the General Assembly. Close to half of all the state senators serving during the period between 1957 and 1975 had spent some time in the House before entering the Senate.[7]

Although the customary biennial turnover in membership diminishes the accumulated experience of the General Assembly, it also helps expand the opportunity for new and relatively inexperienced members to become immediately and deeply involved in the process of lawmaking. In addition to the large influx of new members each session, the part-time nature of lawmaking and the absence of a rigid seniority system tend to perpetuate a fluid legislative environment in which ability can overshadow experience alone. As a con-

    [6] Under the 1970 constitution each state legislative district elects a senator for two four-year terms and one two-year term in any ten-year period. The districts are divided into three groups and the sequence of terms is rotated equally among them.
    [7] To cite three of the largest freshman classes in recent years, nine House members were elected to the Senate in 1973, six in 1971, and fifteen in 1967.

sequence few formal barriers exist to significant participation by legislators in their first, second, or third terms. This dimension of legislative service can be illustrated by past experience. In 1969, 40 percent of all bills introduced in the House were sponsored by members in their first or second terms. Also, during the preceding ten years, nearly 56 percent of all House members in each session had served three terms or fewer. These figures suggest that Illinois state legislators do not have to serve an inordinately long apprenticeship before they can participate meaningfully in the legislative process.

REWARDS AND COSTS OF SERVICE

The obvious question that seems to follow from the preceding discussion is one suggested by both Rosenthal and Lockard — How can a state legislature attract and retain its most able members for more than one, two, or even three sessions?

The *Chicago Sun-Times* offered editorially the following thoughts, which bear heavily on the question at hand:

> Staff, which has been expanding the past few years, will have to expand more. If, as many project, the more frequent sessions and heightened work loads force legislator-lawyers to quit in favor of their practices, then more administrative assistants will need to be drawn from the young-lawyer ranks. Quarters, which fortunately are being renovated and expanded, still will be in part second-class. Consideration should be given to better and more working space. . . . Most of all, of course, serious study will have to be given to upgrading the pay and perquisites of legislators, for as the burdens of legislators grow, the attractions of legislating will have to grow with them. It is not enough to desire public service. Public service must be as honestly profitable as any other professional enterprise.[8]

The editors of the *Sun-Times* are not alone in their assessment of what needs to be done in order to retain able, experienced legislators. Larry Margolis argues in an essay on legislative reform that:

> Legislatures need space in which to do their work, to conduct their business in dignity. The members need better compensa-

[8] "Some Legislative Refinements," editorial, *Chicago Sun-Times,* November 15, 1971.

tion. . . . When you elect a member of the state legislature you are, in fact, asking him to give the most productive years of his life to public service in a very high-risk business. If you do not want him to feather his own nest because he is concerned about how to pay for education of his children after he is no longer in office, you have to compensate him. You can say that it was his choice to run, you did not ask him. But that will not solve the problem.[9]

Professor Lockard, for another, points out that "whatever rewards the legislator receives for his service, they are usually not financial."[10]

The public reputation of most state legislatures, according to William Keefe, does not help either:

Complaints against the legislature are familiar facts of daily civics. *Ironically, whether the indictments are accurate may be much less important than that many people are prepared to accept them.* A little evidence goes a long way. Each specific example of way-wardness, it seems, contributes to the massive generalization that describes the legislature as an institution in decline. In the argot of popular appraisal, a bill to raise legislative salaries is a "salary grab," a vote to block an appointment by the governor is "callous partisanship," a failure to accept the governor's program is "obstructionist," a move to strengthen rule by the majority party is "the most coldly cynical performance seen in years." It is hard to shake the impression that when the legislature goes along with the governor its actions will be viewed as "rubber stamp," and when it asserts itself its behavior will be viewed as "obstructionist." The legislature occupies an unhappy position among American political institutions. Part of the reason for this is that the legislature is not only what it makes of itself but what conventional interpretation makes of it.[11]

POLITICAL AND LEGISLATIVE ENVIRONMENTS

The legislator who does choose to seek reelection finds that he must share his political achievements while individually shouldering the

[9] Larry Margolis, "Revitalizing State Legislatures," in *Strengthening the States*, pp. 31-32.

[10] Duane Lockard, "The State Legislator," in *State Legislatures in American Politics*, p. 115.

[11] William J. Keefe, "The Functions and Powers of the State Legislature," in *State Legislatures in American Politics*, pp. 56-57.

political risks. It makes little difference what his motivation is for running or how he does his job. The fact remains that because a state legislative candidate is so far removed from the top of the ticket, he finds it difficult to insulate himself from groundswells running against his party. Not that it is impossible for a legislator to win against a trend in his area for the opposite party, but it is indeed difficult. A legislative candidate has to find a way of winning some recognition within his constituency, and this task is frequently complicated by a lack of campaign funds and a low level of general interest in state legislative races. Protecting his own career is pretty much the responsibility of each individual legislator. According to Keefe, "He must deal with interest groups looking for new hostages to take, with restless and demanding constituents in pursuit of indulgences, with actual and potential political opponents, with problems of campaign finance, with the nettlesome problems of patronage distribution, and with local newspapers which tar him when they describe legislators as scarcely a cut above scalawags."[12] The existing political ethos of a state conditions the way a legislature functions and what it turns out every bit as much as the constitutional and procedural aspects of the institution.

In Illinois, as pointed out above, legislators once elected do not have to serve for very long before they can begin participating meaningfully in the legislative process. However, as a practical matter, newcomers who wish to take advantage of these opportunities are advised to temper their enthusiasm with discretion and restraint. Like most organizations the legislature is governed by an informal code of behavior which is enforced by informal sanctions. This system is usually uncovered by trial and error and it should be no great mystery to incoming freshmen. As Keefe points out: "The legislature, like all institutions, is not altogether hospitable to its members. Newcomers must find their way around and learn the 'rules of the game.' There are problems of winning acceptance and of retaining it. There are admonitions that the best way 'to get along is to go along.' Here and there the 'logroll' is virtually a way of life — the inevitable *quid* in every *quid pro quo*."[13]

In most instances new members will find that the rules are quite

---

[12] Ibid., p. 68.
[13] Ibid.

similar to those found in business and industry — such as courtesy to other members and deference to older and more experienced members. Newcomers are offered three basic prescriptions for success by one legislator who spent many sessions in the House: (1) attend all committee meetings and floor sessions and work diligently on knowing the important legislation; (2) avoid talking too much and try to speak only on subjects of which you can speak intelligently and knowledgeably; (3) speak up for your district; you are expected to do this. Special emphasis perhaps should be placed on maintaining restraint on the floor during debates and explanations of votes. Most members become particularly incensed when their colleagues, especially freshmen, take to the floor to discuss subjects on which their knowledge is obviously limited. As one member put it:

> A freshman shouldn't talk about everything on the floor. This is a bad thing. They should talk only about what they know. If you've got something you want to express, don't be shy, go ahead and take the floor. But you'd better be damn sure you know what you're saying. If you don't they'll cut you to pieces. A guy, especially a freshman, who shoots off his mouth, will be in trouble with any legislation he sponsors. The other members will give him the silent treatment: he'll be up there trying to get his bill passed and speaking for it, and nobody will say a word or pay any attention to him. You would think he was the only person on the floor to hear it.

There are other rules of conduct which should be recognized if a member is to realize his potential as a lawmaker. They would include such matters as keeping one's word and respecting the views of other legislators. The essential point is that the legislature, above all, is a collection of individuals, and success within that group is ultimately the result of personal factors such as reputation, ability, and personality. Achievement must be based upon the proper mixture of these elements.

STAFF AND FACILITIES

In its report to the legislature in 1967, the Commission on the Organization of the General Assembly stressed that, of all its conclusions, "none is held more firmly or supported more strongly by the many knowledgeable persons who have given us the benefit of their advice than this: Illinois legislators simply lack the tools necessary to carry out their responsibilities in an effective manner."[14] To understand, and perhaps dramatize, why the COOGA Commission felt so strongly about this point, one need only turn to former Connecticut state Senator Lockard's recollection of a constituent's letter he once received: "A constituent once wrote asking me to help him obtain an automobile license plate with his initials on it; he apologized for bothering me, but he wondered if my office staff would take care of it for him, when I had neither office nor staff."[15] This, Lockard says, is merely indicative of a common problem shared by most state legislators, who are without staff assistance to conduct research and investigations, or even to write letters.

Lockard notes that California and North Carolina, in providing well-decorated offices for each member, were notable exceptions to the general rule of the late 1960s. "By not providing desperately needed help," he argues, "the legislature is assuredly undermining its own foundation. Legislators, as a result, are dominated by governors, bureaucracies, and lobbyists, in part because they cannot provide any alternative sources of information for substantiating their independent judgment."[16]

A newly elected member of the Illinois General Assembly will find that some significant steps have been taken to do away with some of the conditions described above. The availability of legislative staff and offices should serve both to help each member become a better legislator and to relieve some of the unnecessary burdens which limit his or her development as a lawmaker.

In addition to a desk in the House or Senate chamber, which traditionally was their "office," members of the House and some members of the Senate are now assigned individual offices across the street from the Capitol on the first and second floors of the State Office Building. Space has also been provided there for one secretary for every three representatives and every two senators. Large con-

[14] Illinois, General Assembly, Commission on the Organization of the General Assembly, *Improving the State Legislature*, p. 77.
[15] Lockard, "The State Legislator," p. 114.
[16] Ibid.

ference rooms for meetings with constituents and others are also
provided in this area. In addition, allowances are made for staffing
legislators' offices in their home districts.

Senior members of the Senate (e.g., committee chairmen) have
offices in the north wing of the state Capitol. Each of these senators
has his own personal secretary, but in the case of committee chairmen, the secretary also serves as committee clerk. The same applies
for House committee chairmen.

The development of legislative staff in Illinois has centered around
each of the leadership offices, so that, while a reasonable complement
of staff personnel expert in given functional areas has emerged, very
few legislators (except for the leaders) have their own personal
administrative aides. Since 1965 the number of these professional
assistants — equipped with advanced degrees in political science,
economics, public administration, social work, and law — has literally blossomed. A member of the Senate minority leadership, in
describing the development of their staff, recalls that: "In 1965
we had two staff assistants and in 1967 three. Right now [1975] I
think we have twenty-five. During the last session we were able to
assign a staff assistant to each of the minority spokesmen on the
committees."

A significant aspect of the staffing pattern has been that since
the beginning majority and minority members have had equal
resources for securing professional help. Qualifications for doing
serious research and analysis are more important than party affiliation, although the chances of a registered Democrat going to work
for a Republican leader (or vice versa) are minimal.

Many of the permanent staff hired at the beginning of the staffing
process were graduates of the University of Illinois, Southern Illinois
University, Loyola, Northwestern, and several other Illinois colleges
and universities, who came to Springfield originally as legislative
staff interns. In fact, the creation of the legislative staff internship
program was the first step taken by the legislature to provide individual members and party leaders with staff assistance. The program began in 1961 in cooperation with the Institute of Government and Public Affairs at the University of Illinois, with partial
funding from the Ford Foundation for a time. The institute directed

the program for over ten years, at which point Sangamon State University took over this responsibility. Every year the Sponsoring Committee, a unit of the Legislative Council consisting of legislative leaders and representatives of participating Illinois universities, chooses sixteen or more graduate students in law, government, journalism, and related fields to serve and study under the leadership in both houses during the next academic year. Interns, who receive academic credit for their service as well as fellowship stipends, perform various research tasks assigned to them to give them insights into the legislative process.

CONFLICTS OF INTEREST

Although members of the General Assembly enjoy certain privileges by virtue of their position as public officials, the parallel responsibilities they must assume are considerable. In the conduct of his office a legislator must generate the public confidence that is necessary to the effective functioning of representative government. Public office, as the saying goes, is a public trust. Whenever the interest of a public official in the normal performance of his job clashes, or appears to clash, with the official's interest in his private affairs, a conflict of interest arises. The conflict may undermine public confidence in an official's conduct. The problem is magnified in a legislature in which the members necessarily rely heavily upon outside business and professional interests.

The existence of a conflict of interest is difficult to determine because there is a gray zone of legislative behavior lying between behavior that is "clean as a hound's tooth" and behavior obviously improper and illegal, involving such things as bribery, embezzlement, and theft. As a consequence, efforts made by the legislature to assure the public of its integrity must maintain a delicate balance between the interests of the public at large and the interests of its elected representatives. The public must be provided with sufficient guarantees without discouraging potential and existing public servants from seeking office. The Illinois legislature has been struggling with these problems for some time and took formal steps to regulate the ethical conduct of its members in 1968, in 1972, and again in 1974.

Illinois Governmental Ethics Act

In 1967 the General Assembly passed the Illinois Governmental Ethics Act, which became effective on January 1, 1968 (amended by P.A. 77-1806, approved January 24, 1972). The act, as amended, is designed to restrict the extent to which legislators may represent interests outside the legislature; to limit the opportunities to use public office for personal economic advantage; and to require legislators to disclose economic interests and relationships that could tend to bring their public responsibilities and private concerns into conflict.[17]

Essentially, the Illinois Governmental Ethics Act contains five sections which apply to legislators and to people close to the legislature. The first is a set of restricted activities, such as lobbying for compensation by a legislator, enforced by fines or prison terms. The second, a code of conduct, prohibits such things as the acceptance of any economic opportunity "under circumstances where he [the legislator] knows or would know that there is a substantial possibility that the opportunity is being afforded him with intent to influence his conduct in the performance of his official duties." The third section consists of a set of ethical principles for legislators, which are intended as guides to conduct and are not enforceable. The fourth section sets forth ethical principles for persons with legislative interests (such as lobbyists) and for persons who are close economic associates of legislators. The final section requires legislators and candidates for the legislature to file with the secretary of state statements disclosing their broad economic interests and relationships "likely to create conflicts of interest."

Campaign Financing Disclosure Act

Public Act 78-1183, "An Act to regulate campaign financing and amending certain acts therewith," effective October 1, 1974, requires all candidates for the General Assembly, as well as all political committees which accept contributions or make expenditures, during

[17] The act as amended also covers members of the executive and judicial branches of state government, as well as certain members of local governmental bodies. However, the discussion in this chapter will be limited to provisions covering members of the General Assembly.

any twelve-month period, of more than $1,000 on behalf of or in opposition to any candidate or candidates for public office, to file financial reports with the state Board of Elections relating to campaign contributions and expenditures. A statement of organization must be filed within thirty days of the creation of a committee. Then, reports of campaign contributions must be filed for the period through the thirtieth day preceding an election and for the period through the sixtieth day following an election. An annual report of campaign contributions and expenditures for the year ending June 30 must also be filed. Whenever a candidate or political committee receives more than $500 within thirty days of an election, notice must be given the state Board of Elections within two business days.

EXERCISE OF SPECIAL PRIVILEGES

Questions of propriety and ethics arise in the exercise of a number of special privileges extended to members of the General Assembly.

Personal Privilege

Under *Robert's Rules of Order Newly Revised* questions relating to the rights and privileges of the assembly[18] or to any of its members take precedence over all other motions except those relating to adjournment and recess.[19] Thus a member may interrupt ordinary legislative business by rising "to a point of personal privilege" to speak on matters that relate to his membership in the General Assembly or to answer charges attacking his conduct or impugning his integrity.[20] As the rule states, the privilege extends only to charges relating to a member's conduct as a member and not to charges concerning his conduct before becoming a member. Nor does the privilege necessarily extend to vague charges in newspaper stories or to

---

[18] These include items such as the organization of the assembly, the comfort of the members, the conduct of its officers or employees, the punishing of a member for disorderly conduct or other offense, the conduct of reporters, and the accuracy of published reports of the assembly's proceedings.

[19] Questions relating to the privileges of the assembly take precedence over those relating to individual members if the two should come into competition.

[20] A member may not interrupt a vote or the verifying of a vote and only for urgent purposes may he or she interrupt another member.

misrepresentation of a member's speeches or acts. This device is used most often to allow members to express deeply felt attitudes or opinions that relate only indirectly to issues or legislation and focus instead on more personal considerations.

Immunity

Perhaps the most significant privilege extended to members of the General Assembly is immunity from prosecution for libel and slander. The Illinois Constitution states that "a member shall not be held to answer before any other tribunal for any speech or debate, written or oral, in either house. These immunities shall apply to committee and legislative commission proceedings."[21]

The Illinois Constitution also provides that "except in the cases of treason, felony, or breach of peace, a member shall be privileged from arrest going to, during, and returning from sessions of the General Assembly." This particular section has only recently been subjected to judicial scrutiny in Illinois, but a similarly worded federal constitutional provision has been interpreted to mean that legislators are immune from arrest only for civil offenses when the legislature is in session or when the legislator is traveling to or from it.[22] The word "arrest" has been given a relatively narrow construction which does not include the service of process in either civil or criminal cases. Thus during a session a legislator would be obliged to accept a summons for either a civil or criminal offense, but could only be brought to trial or arrested for the criminal violation.[23]

In Illinois it appears that a legislator arrested for speeding — a misdemeanor — while on his way to attend a legislative session would have to accept a summons, although he would not have to go to trial until the session had adjourned. An Illinois statute holds that membership in the General Assembly "is sufficient cause for the continuance of any action" when the legislature is in session.

[21] This immunity has been held to protect legislative committee witnesses, and even those people who merely speak out at legislative committee hearings though not called as witnesses or asked any questions.

[22] The phrase "breach of the peace" has been given a broad construction in the federal courts and includes all criminal offenses.

[23] It is assumed here that, since the Illinois provision is almost identical in language to the federal Constitution, Illinois would follow federal doctrine on this point, although this is not certain.

This section is primarily applicable to civil actions but it would probably be considered in minor criminal cases.[24]

INTEREST GROUPS

The idea of a conflict of interest is particularly suitable to the legislative setting, where conflict is the order of the day. The legislature is an institution that intrinsically generates and sustains conflict. The result of the convergence of public and private interests on the statehouse is sketched by Lockard:

> It usually surprises a new legislator, whatever the degree of his commitment to particular or general interests, that the legislature is an arena of swirling conflicts among interest groups, and conflicts of enormous scope and often high intensity. All kinds of organized interest groups — and they are legion — and many *ad hoc* groups formed to fight temporary battles come to the legislature to win special advantages or to protect vested interests. They range from historical societies and conservation groups on the one side to business groups and gambling syndicates on the other. The law can become a significant factor in the success of a particular segment of the economy, and therefore every effort is made to assure appropriate legislative action. This is obvious in contests over the levying of taxes. Industry wants the burden to be on the individual taxpayer; retailers want to avoid the sales tax; particular industries want to cut or eliminate specific taxes on their products; alternatively, they seek the "earmarking" of taxes so that the income from a particular tax will go only to serve the interest of the paying group. In this respect, the combined efforts of the highway lobby have won legislative agreement in most states to limit the expenditure of the returns on gasoline taxes to highway purposes. Sportsmen try to have all funds from hunting and fishing licenses earmarked so that the funds can only be used to regulate and improve hunting and fishing.[25]

[24] Under an old Illinois law, legislators were "exempt from the service of civil process during the session of the General Assembly." The Illinois Supreme Court ruled the law unconstitutional as a violation of the constitutional prohibition against special laws granting special privileges. See *Phillips* v. *Browne*, 270 Ill. 450, 110 N.E. 601 (1915). The court suggested that the exemption would have been upheld if it had applied to others as well, i.e., if it had been a general law based on a reasonable classification.

[25] Lockard, "The State Legislator," pp. 118-19.

Private Groups and the Legislature[26]

Although some lobbyists identify themselves as "the third house," they are more accurately seen as part of the other two. Representatives of private groups are physically part of the legislative life. In 1975, 382 lobbyists registered with the secretary of state's office in compliance with the Lobbyist Registration Act of 1969. Their habits vary: some lobbyists work out of Springfield headquarters, some travel to Springfield for almost every session, others attend only when they have a particular bill to watch. Most lobbyists are, however, well known to legislators; some are former members. They are often friends who share confidence and mutual respect. But their relationship is based on more than a desire for companionship.

The presence of vocal and articulate interest groups in the legislative process may stimulate an atmosphere of "swirling conflicts," but, as James H. Andrews points out, private groups also perform a substantial and creative role by initiating legislation, identifying and creating issues, resolving conflicts, and providing information and research assistance to legislators.

The influence of private groups can be seen in almost everything the legislature does. Why is this so? The fundamental reason is this: if we look at the legislature's business as a whole, and at the activities of private groups generally, we find that these groups perform tasks for the legislature that few other agencies do. First, private groups provide the initiative and impetus for a large share of the legislation that moves through the General Assembly. Second, they indicate and establish the clash of issues out of which the legislature determines its course in many areas of public policy. Third, at the same time they help resolve many of the disputes that vex the legislature, and permit it to set a particular policy. Fourth, they provide a number of tangible services, most prominently that of information.

Initiating Legislation. The role of private groups in initiating legislation is a substantial one. Ideas for bills and even their precise

---

[26] Adapted from James H. Andrews, *Private Groups in Illinois Government* (Urbana: Institute of Government and Public Affairs, University of Illinois, 1965), pp. 5-14. More recently, on June 9, 1974, the *Champaign-Urbana Courier* and *Decatur Herald Review* published a feature-length article by Roger Hughes on Illinois lobbyists. The *Wall Street Journal* of June 6, 1974, carried a feature on the insurance industry lobby in Illinois written by Jonathan Lains and Frederick Klein.

wording quite often come from outside the legislature. The main competitors of private groups in this respect (excluding legislative staff) are agencies in the executive branch of state government, local governments, and occasionally individual constituents. Most bills have their origins in organizations, public or private.

A group normally finds a friendly legislator to sponsor its bill and pilot it through the legislature with the help of the group's lobbyist. Legislators do not hesitate to admit that they handle bills for outside groups. In his "Report from the State Senate," published in a newspaper in his district, one legislator stated, "The bill I am sponsoring for the Illinois Municipal League was voted upon favorably in the local government committee last week, and the bill I am handling for the Illinois state's attorneys will be set up for hearing in committee this week."

Lobbyist and legislator cooperate for many reasons, but in some cases a legislator sponsors a bill because he too is a lobbyist. He may himself be a member of a private group that wants a change in state law. Professional men in the legislature often handle bills advocated by their professional associations. Legislators with financial interests in business regulated by the state often take a legislative interest in those regulations. Other ties between the legislature and outside interests are lawyer-legislators who sponsor or work in behalf of bills that are favored by a client or by the legal profession in general.

Identification and Creation of Issues. Groups not only provide the initiative for legislation, they also provide and stimulate much of the controversy in the General Assembly. They often identify the issues and create them. The lobbyist, with a checklist of matters that are vital to his group's interest, is alert to anything that may affect those interests. If the group is threatened, the lobbyist makes his opposition known. If the group is favored (meaning it probably had the bill introduced in the first place), he supports the legislation. This opposition and support are what the legislature relies on for most of its cues about what the issues are. For the legislature, issues are interests, and the interests it considers at any one time tend to be those called to its attention by organized groups and their lobbyists.

Some interests are represented to the legislature publicly. Lobbyists testify at hearings of House and Senate committees, or officers of the group or business travel to Springfield to do the job. Some witnesses substantiate their positions with careful statements. Others think that little more than an appearance is necessary to indicate their opposition, and this is all they do for the record. Some groups follow the advice of the Illinois Education Association: "Legislators do react to numerous contacts, persuasive arguments, and large audiences. . . . Therefore it is necessary on highly controversial matters to pack committee rooms and chamber galleries." Groups with large memberships may organize letter-writing campaigns. Some concentrate on letters and telegrams to legislators from important constituents and old friends.

Many lobbyists never testify at hearings at all. In looking for interests that are active on a bill, outside observers of the legislature can often report only that they saw a lobbyist in town on the day a bill was voted on.

One of the reasons for referring bills to committees of the House and Senate is to identify opposition. A favorable committee recommendation, if not marred by dissents carried onto the floor, is regarded as evidence that a bill is not controversial, that interested groups favor it or at least do not oppose it. Lobbyists therefore do not object to and even seek committee hearings. Many times a sponsor accepts amendments in committee in order to silence opposition, and a committee may wait to act on a bill until the sponsor and interested groups reach agreement.

Legislators on committees often look to certain groups to keep them informed on certain kinds of legislation and invite expressions of opinion by lobbyists if they are not volunteered. For example, bills involving tax and bond questions in Cook County invariably prompt some legislator to ask in committee for the position of the Chicago Civic Federation on the proposal.

One pattern, then, is for committees to wait for group conflicts to be resolved, approve agreed bills, and send them to the floor. If the conflict is not resolved, members of the committee have at least identified the organized interests they are voting for or against.

The aim of most lobbyists is to maintain their groups' interests without controversy. One way to do this is to avoid attention. Bills are sometimes described by their sponsors as "merely bills" — bills that merely do this or that, bills without substantial effect. If a sponsor can suggest that his bill is not important, except perhaps as a convenience to a group of constituents, he is likely to receive a favorable vote. Legislators will not go out of their way to disturb the atmosphere of camaraderie that pervades the legislative halls. Before the legislature developed its own staff, a lobbyist was always in a better position if he could discourage legislators and news reporters from reading his bill or analyzing it. Doing so might bring opposition. For the same reasons, if a lobbyist wanted to defeat a bill or eliminate unfriendly provisions, the task was often easy. Longer annual sessions and the addition of a full-time professional staff working for the different caucuses and responsible to each of the four legislative leaders (the speaker of the House, the president of the Senate, and the two minority leaders), as well as a limited number of legislative aides working for individual members, have meant that nearly every bill is now closely scrutinized and worked over within the legislature. As a result almost every proposal which would do better if it were not exposed to much public light is now evaluated on the basis of what it is and then amended or defeated. Opposition, whether generated internally or externally, always brings pressure on the sponsor to compromise. Unless a majority has been mobilized in favor of the bill as written, or the sponsor is unusually rigid in his position, the bill will be amended or lost without great expenditure of effort. To pass a bill that has opposition is a job undertaken only for the most serious reasons.

This means that a group wanting to make major changes in state policy in the legislature must do more than undertake a little friendly lobbying. It must overcome opposition groups that have well-cultivated friends. One way to do this is to expand the arena of conflict and bring into play pressures not normally applied in the legislature on a day-to-day basis. A group with this aim may mount a statewide campaign to influence the legislature from the outside. It is obvious that this method can be used only by a group with many members throughout the state who have a strong interest in the group's policy. Beyond that, the policy itself must have aspects that will attract public support. Groups bring the public into their campaigns when they are losing in the legislature.

Individual legislators sometimes encourage demonstrations of group support in order to strengthen their own position in Springfield. Groups without large constituencies or with less popular causes are better off limiting the conflict to within the legislature, where they may be stronger and the pressures may be more manageable. One of the legislators who worked unsuccessfully for the passage of a bill told its advocates later, when they sought support for the same bill in the next session, "The legislature would have more courage to stand up to other interests if school men had more courage to educate their legislators. . . . It's up to you people to see that the bill passes."

Even after groups win initial legislative sponsorship of their bills, they are expected to also provide the margin of support required for victory.

Resolution of Conflict. Private groups not only propose much of the legislation and provide much of the controversy that confronts the legislature, but, paradoxically, they also resolve conflict. In rudimentary form this is what takes place in a House or Senate committee when a bill's sponsor and a dissatisfied group are asked to agree on amendments if they want the bill approved without dissent. A more highly developed form is "legislation by collective bargaining," the procedure by which representatives of two strong counter interests negotiate like diplomats, entirely outside the legislature, and then submit their treaty for ratification. Until several years ago this was the customary method for changing protective labor laws and mining laws, where labor and management were so strongly organized for legislative battle that they could not win unless they agreed between themselves. In this case the work was done by a committee composed of labor leaders and businessmen who were chosen by their respective organizations. They negotiated their differences and if they succeeded in reaching a mutually agreeable conclusion, they presented an agreed bill to the General Assembly. Then, the legislature would invariably accept their recommendations. In recent years this process has broken down as labor has gained stronger support within the General Assembly, thereby invalidating the need for negotiating with opposing business groups outside the legislative arena.

The advantage of this procedure to the legislature was that the law could be adjusted to changing circumstances without the risk of criticism from groups most directly interested. In addition, the legislature did not have to concern itself with the technical complications of these fields of law.

Service to the Legislature. In addition to the basic functions outlined above, private groups provide a number of services that assure them positions of influence in the legislative process. Most prominently, they help meet the continuing need for information. Groups with research staffs have technical competence, often nearly a monopoly in their field of interest, as well as a desire to be helpful. For example, the chairman of an education committee of the General Assembly may call the education specialist employed by an interest group with offices in Springfield. He asks him to compile some recent statistics on injuries to school children while riding in school buses so that the figures can be included in a speech the legislator is scheduled to give on school bus safety. He calls because he wants the information, he knows the specialist has it within easy reach, and he knows the specialist as a friend and trusts him to report accurate information. He may call the lobbyist rather than an official agency because he wants his own source of information or wants to check it with a figure given him by another office.[27] The specialist is glad to help, of course. He is strengthening his reputation for reliability and helpfulness and he hopes he will find a sympathetic ear for his program when he offers it next time. Information is clearly a resource that groups can use to influence the legislature. The lobbyist can sometimes draw not only on the results of a greater research effort, but also on greater technical competence than the legislature can.

Even when information is made available to legislators, however, it may not be read or studied. Rather, it is often used as justification or "cover" for what the legislature intends to do anyway. Even in this respect, the private group is participating in the legislative process.

Groups use many weapons to increase their legislative influence. Several, such as providing information and organizing public campaigns, have been mentioned above. A few more should be pointed

[27] With the development of a professional in-house legislative staff, a legislator now has a means to check on the accuracy of both lobbyists and executive agencies.

out. Groups usually try to establish especially warm relations with committees that customarily handle their bills. If standing committees are unlikely to act favorably on group programs, groups sometimes are instrumental in establishing *ad hoc* committees where interested parties negotiate on more favorable terms. For the same reason, groups that want positive action have favored the establishment of legislative commissions where agreements can be worked out between sessions and presented to the next legislature with all the force of agreed legislation. However, as was described in the last chapter, this practice is diminishing as the committee system becomes stronger.

The role of private groups in the General Assembly, then, rests upon at least two qualities of groups. One is their possession of specific and often technical knowledge in their own fields of interest. This requires the legislature to rely on groups for detailed information and encourages it to look to them for more general suggestions. The other quality is the representative character of private groups. They represent people and interests, and legislatures respect both. For this reason the Illinois General Assembly looks to private groups to recommend legislation, to express opinions, and to compromise with other points of view, all as an expression of the will of their members. Fundamentally, the adoption of a group's program by the legislature can be understood as the legislature's belief that it should serve the wishes of its constituents. The problem is that the legislature has constituents not represented by private groups at all, or represented imperfectly by them. For this reason, justification of group influence as a representative system becomes very complicated. This does not, however, contradict the representative character of private groups as the most basic explanation for their acceptance.

Other Activities of Groups. The most direct efforts made by private groups to establish public policy favorable to their interests are made in the executive and legislative branches. Other avenues of influence, further removed from the final decisions made in Springfield, involve changing public opinion generally, cooperating with political parties, helping to elect friendly candidates, and supporting or opposing statewide referenda and constitutional amendments.

Public relations campaigns to create a sympathetic public for a group's point of view are more commonly used on a nationwide than a statewide basis. Many large groups satisfy themselves with programs to educate their own members. For example, the Illinois Agricultural Association holds county "policy development" meetings to discuss problems of agriculture and find out members' attitudes and interests. A member of the IAA staff attends these meetings to explain the issues in Springfield from the point of view of the group's central office. Many groups publish magazines, newsletters, and pamphlets that articulate group problems and suggest appropriate legislative responses.

Some groups make an effort to work through political parties to achieve their aims. They try to insert their programs in party platforms and may offer their cooperation in other efforts if the party accepts their positions.

Some organizations rate candidates for election in terms of their support for group programs. The Illinois Federation of Labor rewards friendly legislators by publishing flags next to their names in its newspaper, repeating the list in the weeks before election. Labor organizations and other groups go a step farther by endorsing candidates, recommending that their members carry on "the tradition of . . . rewarding your friends with your vote." Private groups and their officers and lobbyists often buy tickets to fund-raising dinners for friendly candidates or act as sponsors themselves. Many groups pay candidates' campaign expenses or make direct financial contributions. In some areas labor unions and their political subsidiaries organize precinct workers to support candidates and party tickets. A few organizations have voter registration and "get out the vote" campaigns.

RELATIONS WITH THE PRESS

Douglass Cater has written:

> The reporter is the recorder of government but he is also a participant. . . . He as much as anyone, and more than a great many, helps to shape the course of government. . . . He can choose from among the myriad events that seethe beneath the surface of government which to describe, which to ignore. He can illumine policy and notably assist in giving it sharpness and clarity; just as easily, he can prematurely expose policy and, as with an underdeveloped

film, cause its destruction. At his worst, operating with arbitrary and faulty standards, he can be an agent of disorder and confusion. At his best, he can exert a creative influence. . . .[28]

There is often a lack of understanding between members of the General Assembly and the press, and this can profoundly affect popular understanding of public issues. A certain level of conflict is inevitable and healthy, but when antagonisms build to the point where the public sees only a distorted and confusing picture of government, some revisions would seem to be in order. One of the functions of a legislative body is to generate the discussion of public issues. Obviously the press plays an important role in disseminating the fruits of that discussion to the public. On a busy day thousands of words flow from Springfield and dozens of "events" occur. In reporting what happens the press is significant not so much for its interpretation of specific events but for its selection of what is news and what is not. The responsibility for the proper selection of events and words, however, does not rest with the press alone. Newsmakers, too, must take some pains to insure that reporters fully understand the significance of events. The roles of reporter and legislator may sometimes conflict but their responsibilities are certainly parallel.

Press relations can perhaps best be understood in terms of daily routines and responsibilities. For ten years Tom Littlewood covered Springfield for the *Chicago Sun-Times*. Below he reports on some of the problems that confront a reporter trying to cover government in a large state like Illinois when the legislature is in session.

> Understandably absorbed in their own activities, few legislators are aware of the magnitude of the Statehouse correspondent's beat. In addition to covering the legislature, he is responsible for reporting on the executive and judicial branches of state government. . . . All this means the conscientious reporter has little time for leisurely reflection when the legislature is in session.
>
> Here, for example is how a typical day in Springfield [when the legislature is in session] might go: First thing in the morning the governor may hold a press conference — and, though it never fails to irritate legislators, the governor commands public attention. Or perhaps the state supreme court is handing down opinions

[28] Douglass Cater, *The Fourth Branch of Government* (Boston: Houghton Mifflin, 1959), p. 7.

which must be digested, translated into English, and, if possible, made some sense of. Then, too, the level of public morality is such in Illinois that a local grand jury may well be dealing with some irregularity of statewide interest that must be followed carefully.

New bills that are introduced once the day's legislative session begins must be screened and evaluated as to their importance and impact. The action on the floor of the legislature must be covered. Stories must be written and transmitted either by Western Union or telephone. And a couple of times in the midst of the literary production an editorial writer or someone else from the Chicago office might call with a question about some legislative happening.

In the afternoon, if the reporter has any stamina left, there are committee sessions. These are often the most significant of all the day's activities. But their prospective importance is difficult to judge in advance. Along with the endless stream of news releases — which, unfortunately, often try to obscure the meaning of the news — there may also be voluminous reports from some administrative agencies or state commissions to scan. In the evening there are likely to be obligatory social events. And, on top of it all, if the reporter works for an afternoon newspaper he has the ever-present "overnight" to file — a story composed in the middle of the night for use the next day.

But time and stamina are the simplest of the reporter's concerns. In any Statehouse the legislator and the journalist who is reporting his activities may be surprised to find themselves sharing a common problem: the difficulty in obtaining reliable factual information about what is really going on. For our tradition of part-time citizen-legislators has meant that the only pros in the legislature are the managerial cliques who profitably preserve their monopoly of insight.[29]

In addition to the three large Chicago dailies and the two St. Louis dailies, the Associated Press (AP), United Press International (UPI), and the Copley Press Service also maintain full-time bureaus in Springfield. Press coverage of state government has increased tremendously in the last decade, another reflection of increasing governmental activity at the state level. When the legislature is in session, the Chicago papers send down additional men

[29] Tom Littlewood, "The Trials of State House Journalism," *Saturday Review* 49 (December 10, 1966), pp. 82-83.

to handle the increased workload. Reporters from some of the state's medium-sized dailies also make periodic trips to Springfield for expanded coverage. For the most part, the smaller dailies and weeklies depend upon the AP and UPI for state government news. Representatives from the Lindsay-Schaub, Gannett, and Copley news services supply their member newspapers with additional coverage. Lindsay-Schaub, headquartered in nearby Decatur, and Gannett, which serves the Rockford and Danville papers, maintain full-time reporters in the Capitol only when the legislature is in session, as do the Alton, Peoria, Quad City, and Waukegan papers. Television and radio stations provide the most dramatic coverage of state government, and their activities in Springfield have expanded greatly in recent years.

Working for the District

The state of Illinois is so large and varied that it is difficult to generalize about the demands each district places upon its representatives in the General Assembly. The Illinois economy is extremely diverse. It ranks high among the fifty states in both agricultural and industrial production. Illinois's diversified economy and high volume of industrial and agricultural production combine to make its population among the most prosperous in the nation.

Constituent pressures will obviously vary greatly over the length and breadth of the state. Representatives from urban and suburban areas are generally more prone to pressures over statewide issues, and consequently their voting records can become fairly significant. Downstate districts, on the other hand, are likely to expect more tangible rewards such as bridge and road improvements. Even here, however, categorical distinctions are not entirely accurate. A representative's relationship to his constituents is likely to reflect his own conception of representation as well as the demands of the district. A job of conscientiously representing a rural constituency is related by a former speaker of the House:

> I get hundreds of requests for favors every session. I get phone calls asking for information. Being a representative, or at least being a good one, is a full-time job. People constantly ask you for help. During the off-session I have to drive to Springfield at least

once every two weeks to do something for my constituents. I have to work with every code department in the executive branch, often finding out information for people or arranging for things like jobs or even special requests on federal matters like social security. In a rural district this happens because you are a lot closer to the people.

In contrast, a senator or representative from the city of Chicago may not have to deal with similar requests simply because most are channeled through the government and political system of the city. This generally leaves the legislator freer to be concerned with other matters. It is not unusual for a Chicago legislator to be "promoted" to the Chicago City Council.

One of the most obvious forms of constituent pressure is the mail that flows in each day. Veteran members tend to downgrade the importance of mail, as evidenced by the following comments made by two leaders in the Senate and the House:

> I've never known a man to be defeated for reelection because of one vote.

> Most mail which comes in any volume is organized by militant groups, and I don't really pay much attention to it.

New members, however, often attach a great deal of significance to the volume of mail received on pending issues.

> I remember a fellow in the House who is now serving in the Senate. He went around a couple of weeks and collected two or three briefcases of mail. We were in committee one day and a very innocuous bill was being heard. The sponsor was a new member and he got up and was explaining the bill and the other member got up and said, "Wait a minute. You say that this bill doesn't mean anything? I want to show you the correspondence I've got against the bill." He got out his briefcase of mail and put it on the desk. The poor sponsor didn't know where to go.

Most legislators, however, take the time to respond to their constituents. Many members use form letters to answer questions and requests, especially if they concern an area of special interest.

With the steady increase in the amount of money each legislator is allowed to spend in support of his district activities (staff, office, postage, etc.), an increasing number of legislators are using part of this allocation for mailing periodic newsletters which report on their legislative activities to their constituents.

As this chapter suggests, service in the Illinois General Assembly is a diversified experience. Legislators come to Springfield to make laws, but in the process they engage in a great number of associated activities.

Larry Margolis comments on the world in which each legislator finds himself immersed for months at a time:

> The legislature must be the arena in which major conflicts are resolved or mediated, and there must be an understanding on the part of the citizenry that the legislature *is* an arena.... As the legislature engages in the process of resolving these conflicts or "choosing among the evils," the public witnesses a very disagreeable scene. Conflict is considered disagreeable. The public doesn't like or understand it and has a low regard for the arena in which it takes place....
>
> A revitalized legislature is independent. It has independent sources of information on which to base its judgments, it has the independent capacity to innovate.[30]

[30] Margolis, "Revitalizing State Legislatures," pp. 28-29.

6

Party and Leadership

Aristotle called politics the master science. By politics I understand
him to mean the official decision-making mechanism in the society.
I think he called it the master science because it is the mechanism
by which all other decisions become possible. Our private decisions,
what we choose to do with that part of our time or our money
which is left over for private disposition, become possible only with
a system in which political decisions can be made.

Larry Margolis, Executive Director
Legis 50/The Center for Legislative Improvement

The most pervasive and, at the same time, the most elusive of all
the elements that influence legislative behavior is membership in a
political party. American political life is organized on the basis of
party. Entrance to politics and subsequent success are achieved
through the two-party system. Regardless of the level of involvement
— precinct, township, county, state, or national — from the outset
a political career is usually intertwined with one of the two major
political parties. The contribution of party affiliation to political
success is likely to vary greatly. The national parties themselves are
merely aggregates of state and local organizations of varying efficacy.
Within the states party effectiveness often runs the gamut from
highly organized, tightly disciplined local party organizations whose
support is essential for electoral success to loosely knit organizations
whose support is completely unrelated to individual success at the
polls. This is certainly true in Illinois, where the Democrats and
Republicans are relatively evenly matched at the statewide level but

where local organizations are often quite unevenly matched and competition is frequently nonexistent.

The categories used most frequently in any discussion of Illinois politics are "Cook County" and "Downstate." "Cook County" refers simply to Chicago and surrounding suburban areas while "Downstate" refers to the rest of the state outside Cook County. This distinction enjoys official status since legislation applying only to Cook County or Chicago has been commonly passed by the legislature. A number of laws have also been passed enabling Cook County and the city of Chicago to conduct elections in a manner somewhat different from Downstate. In addition, the two political parties are organized differently in Cook County and Downstate. The distinction between the two areas does make sense. Slightly over half the state's population is concentrated in Cook County, and a majority of the people there live in the city of Chicago. Even more significant, however, is the difference between these two geographic areas in voting behavior. Cook County, and Chicago in particular, constitute one of the state's most consistently Democratic areas. If a Democratic candidate for statewide office is to win, he must roll up substantial majorities in Cook County to overcome the traditionally Republican vote Downstate. A statewide election in Illinois is essentially a contest between Republican Downstate and Democratic Cook County. Within Cook County the contest is between the Republican suburbs and the Democratic city, where the Democrats need a large vote to carry the county by a margin sufficient to carry the state.

The division of the state into two partisan strongholds, however, tends to obscure some important enclaves of minority party strength. Major Republican strength tends to be concentrated in suburban Cook County as well as in the central and northern parts of the state outside the county. Democratic strength is found in the city of Chicago and in the southern third of the state. The relative importance of the Downstate Democratic vote is overshadowed by the huge party plurality in the city. In addition, the cumulative voting system used to elect members of the state House of Representatives regularly permits a party that is permanently in the minority in a particular area to elect a member of the legislature, with all the perquisites and prestige attendant to holding major public office. If he has the requisite qualities, such a person can become a powerful leader in the state party despite the fact that he comes from an area where his party is far in the minority.[1] This accounts for the existence of a large number of Democratic legislators from Downstate and a significant bloc of Republican legislators from Chicago. Such a situation might not be expected in light of the solidly Republican nature of much of Downstate Illinois and the equally solid Democratic character of Chicago.[2]

"As in most other states," writes Austin Ranney, "each of the major parties in Illinois is an agglomeration of state, county, and local leaders and factions, some with legal status and some extra-legal, holding a variety of ideologies. The nearest either agglomeration ever comes to closing ranks and acting as a single united body is when it campaigns in elections for nominees bearing its label against nominees bearing the other party's label."[3] Generally, the Democratic party is less fragmented than its counterpart, although this certainly was not the case in the 1975-76 biennium. With control of the governor's office and both houses of the General Assembly, the Democrats went through an unprecedented ninety-three ballots before finally electing a speaker of the House with some Republican help. The usual cohesiveness of the Democrats is directly attributable to the existence of a large power base in Chicago, where most Democratic strength is concentrated. The city administration and the county Democratic organization constitute the basis for the state-wide party, and in general the Democrats have much more control over the nomination and election of their members to office than do the Republicans. Only rarely can the Republican party statewide be likened to a cohesive organization — occasionally a strong Republican governor can bring the disparate elements of the party together on a continuing basis.

[1] Since 1960 three House speakers — from both parties — have come from districts where their parties were in the minority.

[2] The partisan composition of the Senate more closely reflects the political makeup of the state than does that of the House. The usual Republican majority comes primarily from central and northern Illinois and from the Chicago suburbs. All but a few Senate Democrats have come from Chicago, although since the 1971 reapportionment the ranks of the Downstate Democrats have grown to the point that in 1975 the Democrats gained real control of the Senate for the first time in thirty-six years.

[3] Austin Ranney, *Illinois Politics* (New York: New York University Press, 1960), p. 23.

Members of the legislature, then, are likely to be associated with their party in a variety of ways depending upon their party's standing statewide and within their home districts. Party loyalty can take on a wide range of meanings. Election to the legislature also means membership in a new form of party organization — the legislative party. The demands and responsibilities of party membership in the General Assembly are likely to be quite different from those back home. The nature of this relationship again depends generally upon the conditions under which a legislator is elected and the position of his party within the statewide political system. Equally important is the nature of the leadership within the legislative party itself. Differences within the parties do exist and factions sometimes develop, but the tugs of party loyalty are strong and conflicts between the two parties are often intense. Beyond participation in differences that periodically split each party, party membership also means an association that will determine a legislator's friends, the nature of his social relationships, the issues he will become involved with, and occasionally the advancement of his career. In this ambiguous way party affiliation takes on a significant role in the legislative process.

THE LEADERS

The Republican and Democratic parties play the major role in organizing the legislature, conducting its business, and providing much of the dynamic force behind the legislative process. The majority party in each chamber assumes control of committee assignments, committee chairmanships, bill referrals, and the scheduling of floor activity. These powers are exercised by the leadership of each party, particularly the majority party. In the Senate the president serves as both presiding officer and leader of the majority party. He is assisted by three assistant majority leaders, who help carry floor debate and also act as whips for their party. The president's counterpart, the minority leader, is usually assisted by two assistant minority leaders. Although party leaders in both houses are officially elected on opening day, usually their election is unofficially carried out at party caucuses prior to the convening of the General Assembly.

In addition to the president of the Senate's rights and duties as an elected senator, which of course include voting, his formal duties,

as prescribed by the constitution and the rules of the Senate, are:
(1) to call the Senate to order pursuant to adjournment (he may
call upon other members temporarily to perform the duties of the
chair); (2) to preside over the Senate; (3) to preserve decorum and
order; (4) to decide questions of order subject to an appeal to the
Senate by any two senators; (5) to state and put to a vote all questions and to announce the result of the vote; (6) to examine the
journal; (7) to clear the lobby or gallery in the event of a distur-
bance; (8) to sign each bill that passes both houses certifying that
the procedural requirements for passage have been met. The president also serves as either an *ex officio* or regular member of a limited
number of committees and commissions,[4] and makes appointments
to various legislative commissions and committees pursuant to the
authority vested in him by either the constitution or the statutes.

Certainly more important than any of these powers is the fact
that the president also serves as the leader of the majority party in
the Senate. On the surface his role may appear somewhat perfunctory, since most of the significant responsibilities are delegated elsewhere. Actually, however, those powers which are not formally delegated to him accrue to him informally. For instance, the president
is not authorized to make committee assignments; that power is
delegated to the Committee on Committees. In reality the president
does make the assignments or has the final word in assigning members to a committee because his caucus will almost always support his
choices for the chairman and majority party members of that committee. Thus, having determined the composition of the Committee
on Committees, the president's decisions on committee assignments
are likely to be affirmed by that committee. Assignment of bills,
another important source of influence, is formally allocated to the
Committee on the Assignment of Bills. Normally, the chairman (who
for more than a decade now has been one of the assistant majority
leaders) is responsible for this daily chore. But here again, the president has a considerable amount of influence and can exert his will
on those few occasions during a session when the assignment of a

[4] Among the groups of which he is a member are the Senate Operations
Commission, the Legislative Council, the Legislative Reference Bureau, and
the Intergovernmental Cooperation Commission. He is also part of the delegation representing Illinois at the National Conference of State Legislatures.

bill to committee assumes critical significance. The Senate Operations Commission is a third major repository of influence which actually accrues to the president. This commission is technically responsible for the hiring and firing of Senate employees and for the assignment of office quarters. These decisions, however, are almost always made by the leader of the majority party, except in the case of minority party employees, who come under the direct supervision of the minority leader.

As a party leader, the president has a number of other significant duties. On major issues he frequently leaves the chair to articulate his party's position from his desk on the floor. He presents party positions to other political figures and to the press. He schedules legislative business, setting the time, length, and pace of each daily session. On occasion he lends his prestige to other members, particularly by cosponsoring legislation. He mends party fences, informally or through the caucus, and distributes rewards according to established traditions. Finally, he keeps the membership informed on the "big picture." In carrying out these responsibilities, the president is clearly the single most influential member of the Senate.

In practice the office of president closely resembles that of speaker of the House. However, the speaker has more formal control of the legislative machinery. He also is allowed to vote and occasionally he may speak out on issues from the floor,[5] although he customarily maintains as much impartiality as possible when presiding over floor activities. The formal duties of the speaker are: (1) to preside at all sessions of the House (like the president of the Senate, he may call upon other members to temporarily perform the duties of the chair); (2) to open the session by taking the chair and calling the members to order; (3) to preserve decorum and order; (4) to decide all points of order, subject to appeal; (5) to decide, without debate, all questions relating to the priority of business; (6) to announce the business before the House in the order in which it is to be acted upon; (7) to appoint all members of committees and committee chairmen (the minority leader designates who the minority

---

[5] When the speaker wishes to participate in debate, he usually yields the rostrum to the majority leader or some other member of the House and speaks on the issue from the floor. His voting switch is on the rostrum, however, and he votes from there.

members will be); (8) to recognize the members entitled to the floor; (9) to state and put to a vote all questions and to announce the results of the vote; (10) to enforce all constitutional provisions, statutes, rules, and regulations applicable to the House; (11) generally to guide and direct the proceedings of the House subject to the control and will of the members; (12) to lay at his discretion any bill or resolution before the House acting as a Committee of the Whole; (13) to sign all acts, proceedings, or orders of the House, and to certify for each bill that passes both houses that the procedural requirements for passage have been met; (14) to have general charge and supervision of the House chamber, galleries, and adjoining and connecting hallways and passages, and to clear them when necessary; (15) to have general charge and supervision over all employees of the House.

Since the speaker is usually on the rostrum presiding, the majority leader assumes the general responsibility for leading partisan activities on the floor. He is nominally the number two man in the chamber's majority leadership. The nature of the relationship between the speaker, his majority leader, his assistants, and his whips, however, varies considerably with changing circumstances and personalities. Together they run the House much as the president and his leadership team run the Senate. They maintain the same kinds of control in a slightly different way over committee assignments, committee chairmanships, bill referrals, the scheduling of floor activity, and partisan responsibilities.

The minority party leaders in each house generally play a much more muted role in the legislative process.[6] They are usually consulted on matters concerning the operation of the chamber and the scheduling of activity simply as a matter of courtesy, while the authority for such decisions rests entirely with the majority party. The minority party and its leaders find their authoritative responsibilities confined mostly to internal party matters. One of the most important powers they have is that of making minority party appointments to various committees and commissions. They are also their party's spokesmen on the floor and in the press room.

[6] The constitution stipulates that the minority leaders shall be members of the numerically strongest political party other than the party of the speaker or the president, as the case may be.

The minority leader in the House is usually more influential than his counterpart in the Senate because cumulative voting keeps the partisan edge in the lower chamber extremely competitive. In recent years, before losing its majority in the 1974 election, the Republican party had the edge in the House, but its majority was never so large that it could afford any defections.[7] Consequently reasonable wishes of the minority party can seldom be blatantly ignored without some kind of damaging repercussion. In recent years the above generalization has applied equally as well to the Senate. During the 1971-72 biennium an even 29-29 split meant that the majority and minority leaders were leading forces of equal size. In fact, after a member of the majority party died in August 1971, the minority leader's party was actually the numerically stronger party. With thirty votes needed to pass any legislation, neither party could act without at least limited support from the other. Thus, the Senate operated much as if it had two minority parties. In the next biennium the Republicans won the one new seat created by the 1970 constitution and gained a narrow 30-29 edge. In the 1974 election, the Democrats turned the tables by gaining a solid 34-25 majority, their first real majority in over three decades. In the past, substantial Republican majorities, such as the 38-19 margin which existed in 1969-70, had limited the Democrats to a secondary role.

THE LEGISLATIVE PARTY

In discussing the political setting of American legislatures, Malcolm Jewell warns: "A student of the legislature might memorize all of the pertinent constitutional provisions, statutes, and procedural rules and still not understand . . . the political base of legislative power. The sharpest contrasts among state legislatures concern their politics and not their constitutional footing or their rules and procedures."[8]

In Illinois the Democratic party is relatively homogeneous and well organized. The major source of Democratic strength lies in the city of Chicago, where a very effective Democratic political organiza-

[7] Before the 1975 session, the Democrats had a majority in the House for only six sessions in the previous fifty years: 1933, 1935, 1937, 1949, 1959, and 1965.

[8] Malcolm Jewell, "The Political Setting," in *State Legislatures in American Politics,* p. 70.

tion controls the city administration and regularly insures impressive Democratic pluralities at the polls. There exists within the party, however, a group of Downstate Democratic legislators who constitute an increasingly more numerous and significant bloc in the Illinois House. Their presence stems from the cumulative voting system and they tend to moderate the Chicago orientation of the House Democrats.[9] The situation is intensified by a sense of mistrust between those from Downstate and those from Chicago.

Cumulative voting, an electoral device unique to Illinois, plays a crucial role in the election of members to the House of Representatives. It was first adopted as part of the 1870 constitution, and the voters of Illinois have twice rejected attempts to do away with this system of minority representation. Both the proposed 1922 constitution, which would have abolished cumulative voting, and a separate proposition submitted along with the 1970 constitution, providing for single-member districts, were defeated. The latter went down to defeat by better than a four-to-three margin on December 15, 1970. An attempt to place the question of whether to retain cumulative voting before the voters again in the 1974 general election fell short of obtaining the more than 375,000 signatures required for the initiative.

Those who successfully fought for the retention of cumulative voting in the new constitution argued that the system gives people accessibility to their representatives and a choice of political opinion even in the staunchest one-party district. Members of the minority party have an elected member of the government around whom the local party can rally. The conflict that results from this system helps create interest in both the future of the party and the government. Cumulative voting has been credited with channeling conflict of opinion into the legislative process because it provides representation from all sections of the state. Since both parties contain members from areas where their party is not dominant, diverse opinions have a chance to reach both party caucuses and proceedings in committee and on the floor. With the majorities in the House historically small, the party leaderships have been forced to listen to

[9] Chicago's domination of the Senate Democrats was once virtually complete. Recently, however, the city's dominance has been diminished by a growing number of Democratic senators from Downstate Illinois.

these opinions and attempt to reconcile them so that their legislative programs can be passed.[10]

The cumulative voting system insures a sizable bloc of Republican legislators from the Democratic stronghold of Chicago, although the GOP legislators from the city have never been in such direct conflict with their Downstate colleagues as have the Chicago Democrats from time to time. The presence of a large number of GOP legislators from Chicago seems to result instead in increased conflict with Chicago Democrats. As one commentator described this situation, "The city's bitterest opponents in the legislature are political enemies from within its own walls, and those camped in the adjoining suburban areas."[11] Indeed much of the partisan conflict in the legislature finds the Chicago Democrats, who control the city administration, pitted against Republicans from within the city and those situated in the adjoining suburbs.

Over in the Senate, the traditional Republican majority that dominated that chamber for over thirty years evaporated following the 1970 election.[12] Thus, the competition that characterizes relations between the parties in the House, and which had been absent in the Senate, has been very much in evidence during the current decade. In spite of this the Senate is basically a much more stable environment than the House. Smallness in size, longer terms of office,[13] and frequent intercameral movement from House to Senate all contribute to the creation and maintenance of a well-ordered and predictable legislative operation.

For most Chicago Democrats election and reelection to the General Assembly are party rather than personal accomplishments. Accordingly, the concerns of party are likely to be crucial to these members in formulating a broad range of legislative positions. The

[10] Larry Kuster, "A Defense of Minority Representation," legislative staff intern paper, University of Illinois, February 1970.

[11] David R. Derge, "Metropolitan and Outstate Alignments in Illinois and Missouri Legislative Delegations," *American Political Science Review* 52 (1958), p. 1065.

[12] Between 1920 and 1974, the Democrats controlled or organized the Senate on only five occasions: 1933, 1935, 1937, 1939, and 1971.

[13] Because of reapportionment and court decisions, every senator had to stand for election in 1966, 1970, and 1972. Nineteen senators had to face the voters again in 1974, while the other forty were required to run in 1976. For an explanation of the staggered terms for the Senate, see pages 23-24.

power base is in Chicago, not Springfield. This is particularly true in the Senate, where at least three-fifths, and as many as four-fifths, of the Democrats who have served during the last several General Assemblies have come from Chicago. In every session the Democratic floor leader also came from the city. Thus, it is not hard to see why the Chicago political organization exerts a more effective influence over Senate Democrats than over House Democrats, proportionately more of whom usually come from Downstate.

For most Republican legislators, on the other hand, election to the General Assembly is largely a personal accomplishment, since the statewide party has little influence over individual success at the polls. Consequently GOP legislators tend to emphasize political power within the General Assembly more heavily than do their Democratic counterparts. The Republican legislator who regularly returns to Springfield generally depends more on himself and his colleagues for direction on issues than on the statewide party. Efforts have been made under past Republican governors and other state officials to provide some centralizing influence on the legislative party. Even in the presence of this kind of influence, however, the Republican party in the legislature has remained a fairly autonomous body, although somewhat less so than in the absence of such influence.[14]

In addition to the differences between the legislative parties that reflect their relative orientations (Chicago or suburban-Downstate) in the statewide political system, there are also differences within each party that generally reflect some basic differences between the

[14] This tendency toward autonomy is illustrated by recent efforts of the Republican leaders in both houses to provide campaign assistance to their members. Starting with the 1966 campaign, the Senate Republican Campaign Committee distributed funds and provided staff assistance to senatorial candidates all across the state in what was generally recognized as an effective maiden effort. The activities of the House Republican Campaign Committee that year were less extensive. One of the major efforts of the House GOP leadership was the workshop held for candidates in September 1966 on party issues and campaign tactics. Workshops were held again in 1968, 1970, and 1972, but not in 1974. Both the Senate and the House Republican campaign committees, financed largely by fund-raising dinners held each summer in Chicago, have continued to provide financial and technical assistance to GOP candidates on a statewide basis. One consequence of these efforts has been that, as they become more and more effective, members aspiring to challenge incumbents for the leadership have complained that such efforts were being made to help those in power retain their positions.

House and the Senate. As suggested above, the cumulative voting system under which House members are elected insures a sizable bloc of Downstate Democrats that tends to dilute the Chicago orientation among House Democrats as a whole. Charles Dunn argues that cumulative voting serves to insure competition between the two parties in the House.[15] Every two years majority control is determined by the results in a handful of seriously contested districts in which two Democrats run against two Republicans for three seats. Under this system, the minority party in a district, with only a slight hope of winning two of the three seats, may find it has two candidates competing against each other rather than against the candidates of the majority party. The system can also result in deflating or inflating a party's share of representation in the House relative to its total statewide vote. Dunn cites the comments of the House Democratic leader after the 1970 election: "If you look at the election returns the majority of the people really did give a mandate for a Democratic House. If it wasn't for cumulative voting, we would have had a Democratic House."[16]

In thirteen out of eighteen elections between 1930 and 1970 (excluding 1964 and 1966), the minority party had its representation inflated. This means, of course, that the majority party had its representation deflated the same number of times. This tendency to overrepresent the minority party in House membership, Dunn argues, dims the prospects of an effective working majority for the majority party. To illustrate his point, Dunn shows that from 1954 to 1970 (again excluding the 1964 and 1966 elections) the average difference between the majority and minority parties in number of representatives was only 5.7.

With the parties so evenly divided neither can afford to lose the allegiance of many members for long, and the pressure for party regularity can build. On the other hand, Dunn suggests, inasmuch as members of the House are more insulated from electoral competition, they may be more inclined to leave their party on a given issue, knowing there is little chance they will be defeated in an election.

[15] Charles W. Dunn, "Cumulative Voting Problems in Illinois Legislative Elections," *Harvard Journal on Legislation* 9 (1972):627-65. Information in this and the following two paragraphs is taken from Dunn's article.
[16] Ibid., p. 649.

With only four candidates running for three seats, the odds of winning in November are extremely high once a legislative candidate survives his party's March primary. This is particularly true in districts where one party has a marked edge over the other.

Possibly because of this lack of electoral competition, "trading with the enemy" has occurred in the past among certain members with some regularity. As Tom Littlewood pointed out in his book *Bipartisan Coalition in Illinois:* "A side effect of cumulative voting for the House, with its virtually guaranteed minority representation, is close party balance and, hence, disproportionate representation for small trading blocs."

The best illustration of this type of behavior occurred in 1961, when a Democratic speaker was elected even though his party was in the minority, 89 to 88. In recent years, however, this phenomenon has been waning, with the notable exception of the 1975 contest for speaker, mentioned earlier, when despite a 101-76 division between the two parties the votes of minority party members were needed to help elect a speaker.

Party Issues

The vast majority of issues that come before the General Assembly do not result in serious differences between the parties. There is, however, a small but persistent number of issues that do cause intense rifts between Republicans and Democrats. Perhaps the most obvious category of bills creating partisan conflicts are those dealing with elections and party organization. They are bills which seem to confer an advantage on one party at the expense of the other. Occasionally the party responsible for the administration of the state or the city of Chicago is subject to harassment by the opposite party. This is a case of the "outs" trying to embarrass the "ins." Another category includes disagreements over broad programmatic issues which are keyed to the traditional differences between the two parties. These are issues of "principle" which are particularly evident in the parties at the national level but which can also become important sources of division at the state and local levels.

In addition to these three broad kinds of issues there is a tendency for partisan splits to occur over bills that seem totally unrelated to party. One former Republican leader in the House related the phenomenon this way: "Only a small portion of the total bills are really partisan issues, but early in the session a sort of fraternal or 'gang' feeling within the parties develops. Members become very gung-ho for the party as the two parties compete against one another. As a consequence many bills with no partisan significance will find the two parties lining up against each other." This particular kind of party split is difficult to predict, since it seems to be mostly a matter of chance and personality rather than design. Occasionally members of the opposite party will refrain as a group from supporting legislation which would be politically beneficial for the sponsor if he is from a marginal district and must stand for reelection in the immediate future. Events of this nature indicate that party affiliation can be rather important in the legislature.

There are several specific sources of party issues or legislation that come to be identified with one party or the other. Each session the governor's party in the legislature is responsible for passage of his legislative program. The administration program is the largest and most significant set of measures the General Assembly considers; it includes most of the plans and aspirations of state government for the succeeding biennium. Various portions of the governor's program do become sources of partisan dispute, but it is not accurate to say that an administration bill inevitably becomes a hot party issue. Quite often this is not the case. Although cities over 25,000 population have home rule, school districts and special districts must still seek legislation to embark on new programs or meet financial crises. Each session the mayor of Chicago usually has a series of requests for the legislature; often they are for additional revenue. The Chicago mayor's party in the legislature has assumed responsibility for shepherding his program through the legislative process. The Cook County Board president also has members of his party either introduce or watch a wide-ranging series of bills to make certain that Cook County's presently unique position as a home rule county is not infringed upon in any way. Each of the independently elected state officials usually has various bills introduced in the legislature. The secretary of state has been particularly active during the last several sessions since the responsibilities of that office have increased very rapidly in recent years. Practically all of the major political officeholders in the state, then, introduce some kind of program for legislative consideration and in varying degree these programs become identified with one party or the other, although they do not automatically become objects of partisan conflict.

Occasionally the party which does not control the governor's office has submitted a legislative program which has served as that party's counterpart to the administration program. These attempts to commit either party to a specific program have met with mixed success even though by now much of the legislation proposed in the earlier programs has become law. In the past neither party has consistently attempted to commit itself formally on a broad range of legislative items. Major leadership in this area has come from the governor and other officers within the executive branch. However, as the legislature has become better equipped with staff and other resources the development of issues and party programs has become a more significant part of the legislative process. This was especially true in a recent biennium when the governor and both houses of the legislature were of opposite parties. Even if the same party controls both houses of the General Assembly and the governor's office, the pursuit of a legislative program developed independently of the governor is, in some cases, still likely to occur.

Party issues become known to the membership in different ways, depending upon their importance to the party. On some bills, such as those dealing with elections and party organization, the leaders do not have to do much to stimulate their party members' awareness of the significance of the issue, since it obviously hits close to home. On many issues, however, the partisan element is not always explicit and a number of devices are employed to communicate party positions. The caucus is the most obvious device; it is reserved for the more significant issues. Sometimes a less direct procedure is used in which the chairman or minority spokesman voices an opinion on particular bills as they are heard in committee and is then supported by the other members of his party on that committee. Members of the governor's staff, who attend committee hearings and have the privilege of the floor, keep their party members informed of the governor's position on pending legislation. An additional cue is the bill sponsor code. If a bill is sponsored by the party leadership, the names of the leaders will appear as sponsors and cosponsors in the

Digest and on the printed bill itself. As one House member remarked, "With any member, if the speaker's name is listed as a cosponsor on a bill, he will think twice before voting against it." Generally the identification of party issues has been less difficult among the Democrats because of the higher level of discipline and organization found there, but that is also changing. Communicating party positions is easier in the Senate because it is a much smaller and more stable body and information is consequently easier to channel.

THE CAUCUS

A caucus is a meeting of party members in the House or Senate for the purpose of making decisions on the selection of party leaders and on other legislative business. The two parties in each house caucus before the first session of each new biennium to choose their leadership. These decisions become official when they are ratified by each house — normally on opening day. Once the legislature gets under way the caucus is used by both parties as an instrument to solidify the party membership on specific bills or questions of general policy. The different ways in which each party achieves this end reflect the basic statewide differences between the Republican and Democratic party organizations. Among the regular Democrats, as suggested earlier, leadership and direction on legislation and general policy questions come largely from sources outside the General Assembly rather than from among the legislative membership itself. This relationship is strengthened by the fact that a majority of Democrats in each house come from Chicago, where election usually hinges upon party support. The inevitable result is a dependence upon and allegiance to party that is relatively unknown among Republican legislators. The presence of a Democrat in the governor's mansion is another source of policy for Democrats in the legislature. Together these two influences provide the party with a wide range of party positions — sometimes conflicting — which must be pursued and defended in the legislative arena. As a result the Democratic caucus becomes a device by which the rank-and-file members become aware of their responsibilities as a party. With policy questions settled largely outside the legislature, the Democrats tend to use the caucus for strategic considerations such as timing and lining up votes.

Among Republican legislators, even when there is a Republican on the "second floor,"[17] party issues tend to be generated from within the membership to a much greater degree than among Democrats. When there is a Republican governor, to be sure, his ideas and programs have a marked impact on the positions taken in caucus. Nevertheless, the party's legislative leadership assumes a crucial role in formulating party issues and directing the membership in their pursuit. A former Republican floor leader offered the following characterization of a party issue: "The party line in the House is really whatever the Republican leadership says it is. It's the consensus formed after all the party leaders have stood up and given their views on the bill in question. By the party leaders I don't just mean the speaker or the majority leader but the guys who are influential veterans and can swing some votes." In this context the GOP caucus becomes primarily a forum for the identification of issues and the formulation of party positions.

House Republicans distinguish between "conferences" and "caucuses." A conference is simply a meeting of the House GOP membership to discuss issues and other problems affecting the party. A conference is called by the leaders whenever they or other members of the party feel the need for party discussion. During the later stages of the last several sessions conferences have been held as often as once a week. The House Republicans resolve into a caucus only for the purposes of voting to bind the party members to vote a certain way on the floor. Binding members in caucus is an extremely rare procedure; the House Republicans rarely caucus on more than half a dozen issues each session. Neither the Senate Republicans nor the Democrats in either house make this same distinction between "caucuses" and "conferences."

In recent sessions Senate Republicans have caucused on an almost daily basis to discuss issues and problems. Again, binding votes are very rare, and the caucus serves primarily as a device to keep Senate

---

[17] Legislative jargon; refers to the location of the governor's office in the state Capitol building. Reference is also often made in the legislature to the "fifth floor," the location of the mayor's office in City Hall, Chicago.

Republicans informed, not only on party issues, but on special problems individual members might have. The Senate majority leader remarked on the floor during the 1967 session that "there has not been a binding caucus action in this or the last session. Since I have become pro tem [at that time the leader of the majority party was called the president pro tem] the caucus has never bound a man against voting his convictions." There have been cases in recent years when neither a governor nor any other elected state official could persuade a legislator of the same party to change his position on a particular issue.

PARTY DISCIPLINE

There are a number of ways in which each party in the legislature generates allegiance among its members. As stated above, the vast majority of bills are not generally considered party matters, but many do have some partisan significance. On these bills the commitment of either party is likely to vary greatly, and the pressures that each member feels to vote with his party will depend upon the importance to the party of the issue in question. Obviously, the most severe threat that a party can use to guarantee the support of a legislator is the denial of renomination. This sanction is at the disposal of only the Democratic party in Chicago, which contributes a majority of the Democrats in each house. The situation is summed up by a Republican legislator: "The Democrats are a much better organized and better disciplined party than we are. They can get at their men outside the legislature and keep them from being reslated." And a Democrat concurs: "The Republicans use their caucus as their principal instrument of party control. We don't have to — we can discipline our men both in and outside the legislature. Denying a member nomination is a rare form of party discipline." Republicans as well as Democrats effectively utilize a number of other pressures within the legislature to insure discipline. Perhaps the most frequent punishment for irregular party support is the denial of a committee or commission appointment, as the following comment illustrates: "The discipline for party irregularity depends on the types of issues involved. One member was kept off committees he wanted for several sessions, but he finally became chairman of the Judiciary Committee. You'll note, however, that this was a committee which is in a position to do the least bit of harm to the party. A member who has left the party at times may be trusted to handle some issues but he will never be trusted to handle something like party organization because of his past irregularities." This story also illustrates the subtle form party discipline often takes.

The pressures that form around irregular party support are informal and highly personal, and they are not necessarily generated by the party leadership. The spirit that develops within each party can lead to resentment against party irregularity. During a recent session two Republican House members voted consistently against the party on certain issues and provoked the irritation of some of their colleagues: "We mostly left the party on labor and minorities legislation but there was no action taken against us. There was, however, a lot of social pressure put on us. The leadership didn't try to do anything, but there was a lot of personal irritation. I imagine that at least ten or twelve members normally voted against our bills because of our irregularity." For most members the personal friction generated by party irregularity can be an effective restraint against this kind of behavior: "A man's popularity diminishes in direct proportion to the number of times he leaves the party. Legislators are social animals. We can sense the cooling off of personal relations with the other members of our party. I think the personal frictions aroused are the most effective restraint on leaving the party."

The extent to which sanctions are used to guarantee party discipline depends upon the size of the majority in the chamber and the political significance of the issue involved. In 1965, for example, the Democrats had an overwhelming majority in the House as a result of the at-large election. At the time party discipline was lax. The Democrats could easily pass anything they wanted and defections meant little to the success or failure of a bill. The situation changed sharply in 1967, when the Democrats were in the minority and the partisan division in the House was again as close as it traditionally is. Much the same turn of events occurred with the Republicans in the Senate, who went from being the majority by a two-to-one margin in 1969 to becoming the minority party in

1971. In the first instance the Republican majority was so large that despite repeated defections, even on major issues, Republicans were usually able to forestall any difficulties in passing or defeating legislation. The 1971 and 1972 sessions proved to be an entirely different ball game. With only one, and later two, defections needed to pass a bill receiving unanimous support from the other side, the partisan stakes became much higher. The Republican caucus of twenty-nine members acted more in unison in 1971-72 than the Republican caucus of thirty-eight did in 1969-70, largely because the numbers dictated that it do so. The Senate Democrats have encountered similar problems. Their united front of 1971-72 crumbled when they gained a 34-25 majority in 1975-76.

Sometimes a legislator can avoid party sanctions for leaving the party on a particular bill if his vote would endanger his position within his district. The party leadership is inclined to accept this situation as an excuse if it is genuine and is not used with great frequency. As one Republican House leader explains: "We will usually accept an excuse based on a man's district. However, we usually know the composition of a man's district pretty well and we usually know whether he is telling the truth about what his district is going to do to him if he votes a certain way."

The relative independence of Republican legislators, all coming from somewhat diverse local organizations, helps explain why GOP caucuses are held so often. If a member is not going to vote with most of the group, the caucus is the place for him to alert both the leadership and his colleagues. In the process of "counting noses" a member may be talked or cajoled into switching sides, or alternatively he may succeed in winning enough votes to his point of view to carry the day on the floor. Occasionally the manner in which a member votes against his party determines the reaction of his leaders and colleagues. A member of the Senate prompted the following remark by one of his fellow senators: "He leaves the party more than anyone else, but he does so quietly, and he's such a nice, likable guy that he usually gets away with it."

In many aspects of the legislative process in Illinois, personality and reputation are often crucial determinants of individual accomplishment. They often outweigh even such factors as party in determining personal success or failure.

EXECUTIVE-LEGISLATIVE RELATIONS

One important reason for legislatures to attend closely to the executive branch is that governors and legislators, as politicians elected to represent the people, have similar stakes in controlling professionals in the administrative departments and agencies of state government. Too often, the professional bureaucracies are responsive neither to the governor nor to the legislature.[18]

As chief executive, chief legislator, and usually the leader of his party, the governor's actions and decisions weigh heavily upon how the legislature performs and what it produces. Two of the major concerns of legislators throughout the nation are the increasing power of the federal government and the dominance of governors and executive agencies.

Growth of Gubernatorial Supremacy

Writing on the changes that have taken place in the relative strength of the legislature compared to the governor, William Keefe observes that the first state constitutions gave the legislatures supreme power while severely circumscribing the powers of state governors. Today, the positions of the legislature and the governor are almost completely reversed, and constitutional limitations, which once applied to the governor, now work to restrict the legislature. Keefe argues that a number of circumstances and powers can be linked to the emergence and development of the governor as a legislative leader. For example, administration bills — a governor's legislative program — are usually the principal bills of almost any session of almost any state legislature. They occupy a major portion of the legislators' time and their success or failure is used as the chief yardstick by which sessions are evaluated.[19]

An important constitutional power of the governor's which allows him to direct the legislature's energies is his ability to call special sessions. The governor's call specifically limits the legislature's workload to consideration of his proposals. Threats of a special session are also

[18] Alan Rosenthal, "The Views of Executive and Legislative Leaders — An Introduction," in *Strengthening the States*, p. 112.

[19] William J. Keefe, "The Functions and Powers of the State Legislatures," in *State Legislatures in American Politics*, p. 57.

an effective weapon for the governor to use in prodding legislative action.

A governor's major constitutional power is his right to veto any legislation passed by the General Assembly and, thus, to stop it from becoming law (if the veto is not subsequently overridden). In Illinois, the 1970 constitution added the line-item reduction and amendatory veto powers to the governor's arsenal.

A further source of power for the governor is his ability to lead the legislature through his authority over budget making. In Illinois he also has the authority now to take the initiative in executive reorganization.

Keefe concludes that:

> The governor's ascendancy is attributable at least as much, and probably far more, to his role as state political leader as it is to legal-constitutional arrangements designed to strengthen the governorship or to limit the legislature.... If a state has a tradition of executive leadership and if the governor is disposed to lead, the resources with which to lead are at hand....
>
> Superior visibility, superior constitutional position, superior staff assistance, superior claim to representation of statewide interests, superior position in the state party organization, and superior access to political resources (jobs, publicity, credit, wealth, prestige, information, etc.) give the governor the opportunity to make his office about what he chooses.[20]

Views of State Chief Executives

The perspectives of various leaders — governors as well as legislators — suggest several reasons why the legislature's role has diminished and how it can be revitalized. At the 1969 Eagleton Conference for fifty of the most outstanding state legislators in the nation, former U.S. Senator Harold E. Hughes, who served as governor of Iowa from 1963 through 1968, called for a new and constructive dialogue between the branches of government and between the levels of government. "We need," Hughes said, "to listen, give ground, eat crow, negotiate, conciliate, and do whatever is necessary to preserve our federal system."[21] Too often, however, as Alan Rosenthal notes,

[20] Ibid., p. 60.
[21] Harold E. Hughes, "From the Governor's Chair...," in *Strengthening the States,* p. 119.

governors and legislators "have talked past one another . . . and have gone to the periphery rather than to the core of issues in contest."[22]

Hughes served three terms as governor of his state. Each term, he faced a legislature controlled by a different set of partisans. First the opposite party controlled both chambers, then Hughes's party controlled both bodies, and finally during his last two years Hughes found himself dealing with a divided legislature. Hughes, drawing on his own set of experiences, observed at the 1969 Eagleton Conference that:

> The apartheid between the governor and the legislature is deeper than party differences. Most chief executives are convinced that the vast majority of legislators do not understand the problems of the executive. Legislators are equally certain that the old man simply does not understand the legislative process. To a large extent they are both right. Beyond a doubt, there is substantial room for improvement in the typical relationship between a chief executive and his state's legislature. Yet this is a subtle matter that does not particularly lend itself to the direct approach. The governor and the lawmakers should respect one another and understand one another's prerogatives better than they do, but if the proper separation of powers is to be preserved, they should not be too fraternal.[23]

With two sessions of the General Assembly behind him, Governor Richard B. Ogilvie of Illinois filled the same role as that played by Senator Hughes when the Illinois chief executive participated in the 1970 Eagleton Conference. Ogilvie also spoke about the existing limitations in achieving better executive-legislative relations and how state legislatures might proceed in attempting to become a more nearly equal partner with the executive branch:

> Understanding the relationship between a governor and a legislature comes from a clearer recognition of the role of each within the broader political system of that state. The governor's role with regard to the legislature has been characterized in Clinton Rossiter's phrase as "chief legislator." But what does that mean? Does it mean that the governor is a broad policy advocate, a spokesman

[22] Rosenthal, "The Views of Executive and Legislative Leaders," p. 102.
[23] Hughes, "From the Governor's Chair . . . ," p. 116.

for people, proponent of public causes and conscience for public needs? Or does it mean he is a major participant in the arena of compromise, a conciliator with sleeves rolled up at the bargaining table? Probably in the real world it means some of both, but the questions for each governor are which role should be played and which role is he permitted to play within the political environment of his state. . . .

Many legislators do not feel a responsibility to seek out problem areas of public concern and to search for solutions. They view their job as primarily that of a judge, reviewing the case or controversy before them, relying on the adversary proceedings of hearings and debate, and rendering a verdict by their votes.

Both those who avoid most issues because of their potential negative voter impact and those who see a passive judicial role as appropriate will, by their legislative actions, prevent institutional reforms in the legislature from affecting the work product. In reality they are satisfied with the work product of a legislature that defers resolution of controversial proposals or innovative solutions to another place — presumably to the executive branch. Until these legislators see their responsibility to their constituents as an active one, legislative reform will be for naught. . . .

The governor is elected by the people, and is presumed to bring to the office public support for his general positions on public issues. And so are legislators. Yet, as time goes on, a great divergence often appears in the relationship between governor and legislators. I have tried to understand why. One reason is that the governor faces not only legislative issues, but the great portion of his time is spent as chief executive, operating the government from day to day. He must make decisions on a vast array of issues about implementing broad policies and managing a major corporate enterprise. Legislators often become so absorbed in the process of decision-making that they have little touch with the realities of the results of the decisions they make.[24]

Although they have not put their thoughts on executive-legislative relations in writing, other Illinois governors would probably agree.

[24] Richard B. Ogilvie, "From the Governor's Chair . . . ," in *Strengthening the States,* pp. 122, 124-25, 128.

7

Bill Passage: Some Elements
of Success

Judging the merits of individual bills is undoubtedly the most difficult task facing members of the Illinois General Assembly. Each
session the range of subject matter with which a member must con-
tend is enormous. In a typical session he or she must vote on bills
dealing with such diverse subjects as barge line companies, bill-
boards, air pollution, county coroners, pinball machines, municipal
library systems, firemen's pensions, oil refineries, fluoridation, highways, quarter horses, and hundreds of other subjects. Not only is
the subject matter diverse, it is often so complex that only a sophis-
ticated professional can fathom its significance. In the pursuit of
understanding, legislators are still somewhat hampered by the lack
of sufficient staff assistance to help translate the complex into the
understandable. With the large number of bills considered each
session, members simply find it impossible to spend much time trying
to understand every bill that comes up for a vote.

Another factor that conditions legislative decision making is the
nature of much of the business transacted by the General Assembly.
In each session there are only a few bills that stimulate widespread
interest. They make the headlines and are followed closely by the
press as well as the party leadership, interest groups, and agencies
of government. This general attention and the discussion it generates
help to clarify the issues involved. When it comes time for the legislature to take action on these bills, the decisions are relatively easy

to make — primarily because the membership knows what the issues are and can act accordingly. Generally speaking, the more important the bill, the more likely the voting pattern on it is predetermined. However, most of the bills considered by the legislature do not fall into this category. Most bills are introduced to solve problems in a single district or for a special interest group. Having only a limited impact, they arouse little interest outside the circle of those directly concerned. Most members feel little compulsion to spend time investigating a bill which has significance for groups or individuals far removed from the concerns of these members' own districts and constituents. Yet these "little" bills make up the bulk of the legislative workload, and each member of the legislature must voice his approval or disapproval for the record. It is the "little" bills that we are primarily concerned with in this chapter.

Since information is such a limited commodity in the legislature, the content of a bill is often a secondary consideration in the determination of its success or failure. More important are the people who make up the legislature itself. On those issues that do not directly concern them, most legislators are content to be guided by the judgment of colleagues whom they consider reliable, informed, and intelligent. Within each chamber there are a number of individuals who are conceded to be experts or specialists in specific subject areas or simply possessors of broad political savvy. Within their spheres of expertise, these legislators are often relied upon for judgments on the merits of legislation. Thus, an intricate network of personal relationships provides the environment within which most daily legislative decisions are made.

Perhaps because legislators do rely so heavily upon each other in making decisions, over the years they have developed the habit of giving most bills the benefit of the doubt. Bills that do not involve partisan considerations are usually judged innocent until proven guilty. This means that passage will usually be forthcoming if the sponsor can demonstrate that his or her bill has no significant opposition. Legislators are almost eager to help out colleagues in their attempts to cope with the problems of their districts — and they expect the same consideration in return. Each sponsor usually tries to capitalize on this spirit of acceptance by exaggerating the local nature of his bill, its limited impact, and its lack of opposition. If he can successfully represent his bill as having these qualities, then its chance of passage is excellent. It is this fraternal attitude that characterizes much of the committee and floor activity in the General Assembly.

The tendency to move bills along in the absence of opposition is probably most evident in committee. Only occasionally will any standing committee take exception to a sponsor's desire for a favorable recommendation. In most of these instances the bill is of partisan interest or has aroused the concern of an influential interest group.

Yet the fraternal disposition to act favorably on a colleague's bill by no means guarantees passage. There are other factors relevant to a legislator's success in committee and on the floor. Perhaps foremost is his personal standing among the membership. Reputation is often a critical determinant of personal success in the General Assembly. The amount of advance work done by the legislator is also important — not only his probing the membership for some indication of their receptivity to lining up votes, but simply his being prepared to present the bill intelligently on the floor or in committee and being able to answer questions without difficulty. Even if the groundwork has been carefully laid, the legislature may simply not be in the proper frame of mind to pass a particular bill at a particular time. These and other factors constitute the background against which members of the General Assembly make their decisions.

THE SPONSOR

The chief sponsor of each bill plays the most important role in moving that bill through the legislative process. For the most part momentum is generated and sustained by individual legislators rather than by committees, political parties, or interest groups. This is not to say that inspiration for every piece of legislation comes from the sponsor, nor does it suggest that sponsors are unresponsive to pressures from interested parties. Rather, within the General Assembly it means that custom dictates that, upon introduction, a bill belongs to its sponsor. "It then becomes his duty alone," according to one veteran, "to see that that bill becomes law." In such a system bills easily become synonymous with their chief sponsor and are identified more by sponsorship than by content. Consequently, for the sponsor, defeat may be equated with rejection by his colleagues and passage with their approval.

The sponsor is a crucial part of the legislative process primarily because of the exceptional amount of control he exerts over the destiny of his bill. From the point of introduction his wishes are customarily followed in the processing and scheduling of his legislation. At only a few places on the path to final passage is the progress of his bill in the hands of some other legislative agency. Committee referral is usually not a critical step since only a small percentage of bills are actually killed as the result of an unfavorable committee report. Although a bill may end up in a subcommittee or on an interim study calendar, it still is alive and has a chance at eventual passage. Even so, the sponsor can often exert informal pressure for a specific committee referral if he feels the need. Once the bill has been assigned, the committee chairman will usually try to honor the wishes of the chief sponsor. When a bill is finally reported out of committee, the sponsor usually has the prerogative, within the rules of his chamber, of determining when his bill will be called for second and third readings.

Overall, this scheduling power provides the sponsor with considerable flexibility and control over his bill.[1] The extent of this flexibility becomes more apparent when it is compared with the procedure in the U.S. Congress. Once a bill reaches the committee stage in Congress, the original sponsor is left with little authority to influence its progress. Congressional committee chairmen are the individuals who determine if, when, and how bills referred to their committee are considered. Quite often the chairman manages a com-

---

[1] The legislative timetable limits the sponsor somewhat in scheduling the progress of his bill. For example, the April deadlines for introduction of bills, which have been enforced with substantial regularity, have helped to eliminate a tactic common in preceding sessions. Many legislators would wait until the closing weeks of the session to introduce bills or else wait until the closing days to call them for passage, hoping to add them unnoticed to the enormous flood of bills passed in the last chaotic week before the June 30 adjournment. As discussed earlier, other deadlines concerning floor action and final passage of bills, as provided for in the House and Senate rules, have also helped to eliminate this tactic and to make the legislative workload less oppressive and unwieldy. A third factor which has worked against legislators who try to follow this course is that with annual spring and fall sessions both houses have been carrying over a great many bills from one session to the next.

mittee bill on the floor or designates another member of the committee to perform that task. A second and equally significant scheduling agency in the U.S. House is the Rules Committee. The Rules Committee is a standing committee that provides special rules under which bills are debated, amended, and considered on the House floor. It controls the flow of legislation from committees to the floor. In the Illinois legislature a sponsor can be almost a one-man scheduling agency. He, for the most part, is the key to the success or failure of his bill provided he meets all the appropriate deadlines set forth by the joint rules. Once the deadline in April passes, the Rules Committee in each house begins to assume significance — all bills introduced after this deadline are referred there first.

Within the General Assembly, then, individual legislators are blessed with two substantial advantages in achieving legislative success, that is, in getting their bills passed. First, the legislature as a whole is disposed to pass legislation, especially when the sponsor can demonstrate that his bill is relatively innocuous. Second, the sponsor of each bill has broad discretion in advancing his bill through the legislature, including the second house, and ultimately through the governor's office. These two factors in themselves give the individual legislator a formidable edge in getting his bill to the governor's desk. But, as emphasized above, the General Assembly is not a static and impersonal environment. In maximizing his initial advantage, each sponsor must also consider the network of human relationships that make up the legislature. As one state senator remarked, "Without a doubt the simple art of getting along with people is important to any legislator. No one has a copyright on that art, but it is as important to a legislator's success as it is in any business or profession."

Generating Support

Bringing a bill from introduction to a favorable vote on third reading typically includes two major steps. Initially, the sponsor, depending upon his degree of commitment to the bill, makes a concerted effort to generate enough support for it so that by the time it reaches third reading the prospects for passage are relatively bright. He hopes that these preliminary moves will prepare the way for a favorable reception by the membership, but the voting stage itself can be just as critical as the initial efforts to secure a passable bill. Deciding when to call the bill, how to present it on the floor, and what procedural tactics to use are all important, in varying degrees, to gaining a successful vote.

Generating support for a bill before consideration in committee or on the floor can be done in several ways, depending upon the nature of the bill. Usually it is a good idea, as one legislator suggests, to contact personally those parties who will be dealing with the bill as it progresses through the legislature as well as anyone likely to be affected by it: "Legislation to be introduced will have an easier road if discussed beforehand with leaders or chairmen of committees likely to be involved. Successful legislators usually have laid the groundwork for their bills by broaching matters with friends and influential colleagues, both before committee hearings and before call-up on the floor."

The subject matter of the bill usually dictates whom the sponsor should talk to before committee hearings and a floor vote. On many bills it is merely a question of conferring with committee chairmen, influential members of the committee, party leaders, and any individual members of the legislature who might have some interest in the bill. On other bills, it may be necessary to check with those private interest groups or agencies of government affected by the bill. In addition, there are several permanent legislative commissions — such as the Pension Laws Commission, the School Problems Commission, and the Motor Vehicle Laws Commission — whose opinions within their areas of expertise, if not always authoritative, can be assets in the legislative process. A legislator sponsoring a bill that comes within these areas of expertise should at least discuss the bill with the appropriate agency. Agency approval can then be used in committee and on the floor in building support.

The object of this preliminary maneuvering is not only to elicit support, but also to isolate opposition. The tactical implications of knowing where trouble might arise are fairly obvious. In the absence of opposition, most bills will move successfully through committee and be passed on the floor. It is in the definite interest of the sponsor either to eliminate opposition before committee consideration or a floor vote or else to be prepared to counteract it.

In order to develop a passable bill the sponsor might have to change his original bill to accommodate the opposition. This is certainly in keeping with the nature of the legislative process. Lawmaking is a piecemeal process in which results are often incomplete, partial steps toward the solution of continuing problems. Legislators must often settle for less than perfection. In the words of one commentator, "It is the legislator's function to deal in half loaves." Compromise and conciliation can occur at any time between introduction and passage. The sponsor as advocate is in the position of keeping his bill intact as well as getting it passed. During the process, he may well have to settle for a half loaf.

COSPONSORS

In addition to contacting interested parties, the sponsor may attempt to develop broad support by encouraging colleagues to join him in cosponsoring his bill.[2] Most legislators feel that multiple sponsorship is a good way to solicit commitments from other members. It is usually expected that the cosponsors of a bill will support it in committee and on the floor. Lining up sponsors can be done before introduction or on the floor as the bill is being introduced. One state senator stressed that on bills of special importance to him he often tries to get as cosponsors the leaders of his party as well as the chairman and selected members of the committee to which it is likely to be assigned. It is expected that in requesting cosponsorship the chief sponsor will accurately represent what the bill does. However, one member of the House suggested that caution should be exercised in being placed on bills as a cosponsor: "You can really get burned that way if you're not careful. You can easily overextend yourself on these things. After a while in the House, I learned to contain my enthusiasm for cosponsoring bills. It's a real shock to find out later that you cosponsored some long-forgotten bill that comes back to haunt you." The sponsor who misrepresents his bill is not likely to be looked upon favorably by his colleagues.

[2] Cosponsoring a bill in no way gives cosponsors any substantive control over the bill. See Frederic H. Guild, "Co-Sponsorship of Bills in the Illinois General Assembly," *Public Affairs Bulletin* (March-April 1971), for a more thorough study of cosponsorship and the impact it has had on ultimate passage of bills introduced in the Illinois legislature.

In addition to cosponsors in the house of origin, a sponsor must be secured in the other chamber.

REPUTATION

In successfully negotiating the legislative process, a sponsor's most valuable asset can be his reputation. It can also hang like an albatross around his neck. Unlike the other factors that influence the fate of legislation in the General Assembly, a member's reputation is relatively constant and unchangeable. A legislator's personal qualities and his stature as a lawmaker constitute the first things considered by his colleagues as he goes about eliciting their support. It is often the paramount consideration, as one legislator emphasized, in a legislative body where "one simply relies to a great degree upon the integrity of his colleagues in the advancing of legislation." The following comments by two members of the legislature shed some additional light on this facet of the legislative process. One noted: "If there is any one area which makes bill passage easy or difficult, it is the personality of the individual calling the bill. Some people's judgment is generally respected in certain areas, and the Senate is not likely to question a bill in a respected legislator's area of specialty. Other legislators are suspect and, consequently, their bills are examined more carefully. Legislators such as —— , who has specialized in educational matters for more than thirty years as a member of the House, find immense respect on both sides of the aisle." The other legislator added: "Usually you can trust the judgment of most of the members on certain kinds of bills. But it takes time to know who can be trusted on what bills. You've got to study a man for a couple of sessions before you can size him up and be sure you know when he knows what he's talking about."

TIMING

In bringing his bill to a floor vote, the sponsor has to consider the element of timing. "The decision as to when to call a bill is a most important one," recalls a former state senator. "There seem to be days on which a bill must be very objectionable to be turned down. Somehow or other you can sense the feeling of the Senate on a particular day, and you can tell whether or not it is appropriate to call a bill." A proper sense of timing means the ability to call one's bill for passage at a time when the atmosphere of the chamber is conducive to passage, when the members are in a good mood and well disposed toward each other. It is a sense that comes only with experience, and it manifests itself in different ways. As one legislator noted: "If the bill is a nonpolitical one, it is better to call it on a day on which there is not a great deal of disharmony between the two parties. Tempers rise and you may find that you lost some support simply because of a previous heated debate on a party bill." Another lawmaker made this comment: "I called a lot of my bills last session on Monday morning. The members then are well rested and refreshed from a weekend away from this place. They haven't spent any time in committee or on the floor getting mad at each other and the atmosphere is relaxed and pleasant."

Because of the difference in the size of the two chambers and the methods employed to call bills, it is easier to capitalize on the element of timing in the Senate than in the House. In the Senate the president simply goes down the list of bills on the calendar in numerical order and asks each sponsor whether he wants his bill called. It is obvious that the sponsor can take advantage of what he feels is the proper atmosphere by allowing his bill to be called then, or if he feels that he should wait for a more propitious moment he can easily postpone calling it. Of course, the sponsor has to be certain that he will get another chance to call his bill before a deadline passes and it is tabled.

In the House the procedure for calling bills is generally the same, except that at his discretion the speaker may call in sequence bills or resolutions pertaining to the same subject, or he may call bills in the order in which they will be tabled under the House rules. A House sponsor is likely to know whether any hot partisan issues will be coming up that day, but he is not really in a position to fully anticipate the atmosphere of the House, nor can he capitalize on any significant changes in the same way that members of the Senate can. Within the limits allowed him, however, a House sponsor can still pick his spots with some accuracy if his legislative experience has instilled in him a "feel" for the process of timing.

EXPLANATION

Most legislators consider timing and the sponsor's explanation of a bill to be the most important factors at the voting stage. Preparation and presentation are the crucial elements in the explanation of a bill. If the sponsor spends a reasonable amount of time researching his bill and anticipating questions, then he can be reasonably sure of himself on the floor. At the very least it is important to project the image — if not the substance — of knowledge. But the safest way to look knowledgeable on the floor is to be knowledgeable. As Duane Lockard points out, the legislator "needs to know what other jurisdictions have done when faced with the problem with which he is wrestling, what have been the consequences of a particular law in other states, what rationale can be found for a proposal that he wants to make, or what may be the costs and implications of a proposal urged by the state bureaucracy or an interest group."[3] If the sponsor becomes ill at ease, he arouses the attention and possibly the animosity of his colleagues. The membership appreciates a smooth and precise explanation. It saves time and reassures them that the sponsor is presenting a good bill. They also like to think that the sponsor has been doing his homework and taking the business of lawmaking seriously. As a former member of the General Assembly observed: "Doing homework is important. Knowledge of the subject matter is always vital, and if one gets a reputation as a legislator who just does not dig deeply into any given subject, his effectiveness as a legislator correspondingly diminishes."

A good bill explanation in the General Assembly is one which is straightforward and brief. The object is to stand up, explain the bill, and hope that everyone is satisfied. A veteran lawmaker explained:

> Many bills get talked to death. When the sponsor could have passed the bill, he talked too long about the bill and raised doubts which might not have previously existed. If the bill is basically simple, the explanation should be short and simple with an expressed willingness to explain any sections that may not be understood.

[3] Duane Lockard, "The State Legislator," in *State Legislatures in American Politics*, pp. 123-24.

I have found that the more concise and brief you are in explaining a bill on the floor, the better off you will be. That is, be prepared to answer any questions which may be proposed to you, but don't elicit questions by long-winded explanations. This lesson came a little late for me. As a lawyer, I had assumed that when I first came to Springfield a rational explanation of what a certain bill did was desired. Such is not the case. As a practical matter, considering the tremendous lack of time and tools under which every legislator labors, it is not surprising.

A basic knowledge of the rules of procedure can prove to be an additional asset at the point of explanation. This kind of knowledge is helpful in making a smooth presentation and in bolstering a legislator's confidence. While a few members in each house are respected as expert parliamentarians, parliamentary skills are not usually basic to success. They can be useful but are not exceptionally significant. Once in a great while they can be used to achieve an otherwise difficult goal.

This discussion does not presume to exhaust the intricacies of legislating in the Illinois General Assembly. It is presented only to suggest some of the more critical junctures in that process and also to illustrate some of the determinants of legislative success. It must be emphasized that the bills referred to here are the less controversial measures that constitute the bulk of the legislative workload. Toward such bills the legislative environment is usually receptive. Each sponsor begins with bright prospects for eventual success. He is also in a position to enhance these prospects at several points along the path from introduction to passage. Some of the major methods employed by members of the legislature to achieve this end have been suggested. An attempt has also been made to illuminate some of the more ambiguous aspects of lawmaking. Getting a bill passed can be an almost perfunctory process. On the other hand, it can be a frustrating effort dependent upon conditions very difficult to anticipate.

8

A Bibliographical Essay on
the Illinois General Assembly

In the bibliographical listings at the end of this chapter we have tried
to include all major works dealing with the Illinois legislature. Some
of the more significant of these works are summarized below. Not
included here is the general literature on state legislatures, a previously sparse but now growing body of work. Citations to some of
these materials appear in the footnotes to previous chapters of this
book.

Comprehensive books dealing specifically with the Illinois General Assembly are almost nonexistent. The one exception is Gilbert
Y. Steiner's and Samuel K. Gove's *Legislative Politics in Illinois*
(1960), which is now dated and out of print. This work is a descriptive study of the legislative process in Illinois and the factors
which operate in that process.

David Kenney's *Basic Illinois Government* (rev. ed., 1974) presents an excellent overview of the entire state government, including
its history. The approach tends to be descriptive, with a reform bent,
rather than analytical. The book has an excellent list of references.

Thomas Littlewood's *Bipartisan Coalition in Illinois* (1960) is a
detailed, often fascinating account of the contest for speaker of the
House of Representatives in the 1959 session, which resulted in the
victory of Paul Powell, a "minority" candidate. It also is quite dated.

Another informative case study of Illinois legislative politics was
conducted by John P. Heinz *et al.* Published in the *Northwestern
University Law Review* (1969), this study is based on the "elitist"

model of political systems. Because the study deals with only a few bills on criminal law, the systematic general hypothesis which the authors put forth is extremely difficult to substantiate. The authors argue that the Illinois General Assembly is controlled by a group of elites. At the same time they present evidence to confirm this point, the authors emphasize that these elites must often carefully consider public opinion before acting. Hence, they are indirectly accountable to the general public. Although limited in scope, both this study and Littlewood's book should be required reading for anyone seeking a working knowledge of the General Assembly.

Works such as the Steiner and Gove book were written as studies of the legislative process; they were based on personal observation of the legislature. Of perhaps less value to the student of Illinois government are the behavioral studies of the General Assembly which are based solely on the records of roll call votes. Two of the best known are David Derge's "Metropolitan and Outstate Alignments in Illinois and Missouri Legislative Delegations," a study published in the *American Political Science Review* (1958), and William J. Keefe's "Party Government and Lawmaking in the Illinois General Assembly," which first appeared in the *Northwestern University Law Review* (1952). In the former study Derge compares the frequency of Chicago-Downstate voting assignments with party voting in the General Assembly, and also explores the apparent degree of cohesion within different blocs of the legislature. Keefe's article is an earlier study of the frequency of party votes in the legislature and of the types of issues likely to elicit them. Because the article was written almost twenty-five years ago, however, some of the author's findings now lack the validity they once had. Another study focusing on the behavioral aspects of the legislative process in Illinois is Frederic H. Guild's "Behavioral Patterns for Handling the Legislative Workload," a paper issued in 1968 by the Public Affairs Research Bureau of Southern Illinois University. Using a computer, Guild catalogued the numerous ways in which the General Assembly attempts to cope with the large number of bills considered each session.

Another work on Illinois government, by Thomas J. Anton, describes and analyzes the role of the General Assembly in the state appropriations process, and also provides a detailed view of the functioning of the entire appropriations apparatus. Anton's book *The Politics of State Expenditure in Illinois* (1966) presents a critical view of the legislature's ability to control state appropriations. This book has been dated by changes on both the legislative and the executive sides. Glenn W. Fisher's *Taxes and Politics* (1969) analyzes the state's revenue system in considerable depth. It has some references to the role of the legislature in determining tax policy.

Perhaps because their activities are so salient a feature of the legislative process in Illinois, lobby and pressure groups have been fairly well covered by writers on the legislative process. In addition to the analysis of lobbies in Steiner and Gove, useful discussions can be found in George Hoffman's *University of Illinois Law Forum* article "The Lawyer as a Lobbyist" (1963) and in James Andrews's *Private Groups in Illinois Government* (1965). Hoffman's article is a limited, but interesting, discussion of the activities of lobbyists in initiating legislation and working with legislators. Unfortunately, Hoffman cites no examples to reinforce his description. Further discussion of the role of lobbies in the legislature is provided in Andrews's work, which emphasizes the concept of the legislature as a passive framework responding to pressures, a concept previously developed in the literature on state legislatures.

The significance of cumulative voting to the legislature is explored in George S. Blair's 1960 study, *Cumulative Voting: An Effective Electoral Device in Illinois Politics*. Blair compares the Illinois House to the lower houses of four other states to see whether cumulative voting has any effect on turnover rates and other characteristics. Although he does offer some criticisms of the consequences of cumulative voting, Blair's overall evaluation of its use is favorable. A more recent study that tends to put cumulative voting in a negative light is Charles W. Dunn's "Cumulative Voting Problems in Illinois Legislative Elections" (1972). A basic description of election procedures, as well as geographic voting patterns and party strength, is given in *Illinois Politics,* by Austin Ranney (1960).

The question of legislative reapportionment in Illinois has been the subject of numerous articles and studies. The most recent comprehensive publication in this area is James L. McDowell's *The Politics of Reapportionment in Illinois* (1967). McDowell's book is essentially a case study which chronicles reapportionment activities from 1953 on. The material was later updated and expanded in the author's unpublished 1972 doctoral dissertation. Although it is a detailed account similar to Littlewood's *Bipartisan Coalition in Illinois,* McDowell's book does not quite match the former study's close-up view of legislative decision making. Nevertheless, his book is the most comprehensive account in this area, and provides an ample frame of reference for understanding the politics of redistricting. "Reapportionment and Illinois Public Policy," a 1966 article by Samuel K. Gove in the *Illinois Business Review,* also deals with the history of reapportionment in Illinois, and discusses its possible impact on future behavior in the legislature. In a later monograph, *Reapportionment and the Cities: The Impact of Reapportionment on Urban Legislation in Illinois* (1968), Gove analyzes the relationship between reapportionment in Illinois and the involvement of the General Assembly in the problems of the cities. He concludes that "reapportionment has had little effect on the urban legislative product."

To understand a legislature which responds to public opinion, it seems necessary to have some idea of the type of information about the legislature which is being presented to the public. Several pertinent studies of the press coverage of the General Assembly have been made, and perhaps the most extensive of these is "Newspaper Portraits of the General Assembly," an unpublished master's thesis by Douglas Kane (1967). Kane's thesis centers on a discussion of the different types of coverage of the General Assembly by major Illinois newspapers. It gives considerable insight into these newspapers' selective reporting of different events and the "slanting" of news which results. Another study on this same subject is the unpublished doctoral dissertation of Richard Hatch (1969). Entitled "Reporters and Legislators in Illinois: Their Roles and How They Interact," Hatch's study closely examines the interaction between legislators and legislative correspondents.

In recent years a large amount of criticism from both public and private sources has been leveled against the operation of the General Assembly as inefficient and in need of change. In response to this, the 1965 session of the legislature created the Commission on the Organization of the General Assembly, which studied the operations of the legislature between 1965 and 1967 and produced a comprehensive program of recommendations for changes. *Improving the State Legislature,* the final report of the commission, summarizes these recommendations and discusses the problem areas which initiated them. The report deals with changes in floor and committee procedure, legislative facilities and staffing, and the operation of the appropriations system with respect to the General Assembly. Representing the conclusions of a group of experienced legislators and academic experts, the report is significant because it discusses shortcomings of the legislative institution which have been identified by the members of the institution themselves. Although no model for an ideal General Assembly is presented, a fragmented picture of the legislators' conception of their proper role is obtained from the report. The commission report is also valuable as an indicator of the path which change in the General Assembly will take.

A more recent analysis of the Illinois legislature is found in the Citizens Conference on State Legislatures' *State Legislatures: An Evaluation of Their Effectiveness* (1971), summarized in *The Sometime Governments* (also published in 1971). In January 1976 the Citizens Conference changed its name to Legis 50/The Center for Legislative Improvement.

As mentioned throughout the text, the 1970 constitution has brought about many changes in the Illinois General Assembly. The convention and its committees generated numerous reports. The Legislative Committee's report is now published in volume VI of the *Record of Proceedings of the Sixth Illinois Constitutional Convention.* The committee also issued a separate report, "Legislative Article: Comparative Information," which was not published in the *Record of Proceedings* of the convention. Separate sections are devoted to unicameralism, cumulative voting, the size of the General Assembly, qualifications and powers, and apportionment.

Many publications have analyzed the convention and its work. On the legislative article, Charles Dunn has written "Future of Legislative Reform in Illinois: The 1970 Constitution," which appeared in the *Chicago Bar Record* (1971). William Hanley has analyzed the governor's new veto powers in "The 1970 Illinois Constitution and the Executive Veto," a 1972 paper issued by the Public Affairs Research Bureau of Southern Illinois University.

Newest on the scene is *Illinois Issues,* a monthly magazine devoted to state government. Since publication began in January 1975, several relevant articles on the legislature have appeared.

BIBLIOGRAPHICAL LISTINGS

Operation and Procedure

Arrington, W. Russell, and Richard E. Dunn. "Governmental Evolution and the Response of State Legislatures." *State Government* 43 (1970):174-78.

Burditt, George M. "The Birth of a Bill — Illinois Legislative Procedures." *Chicago Bar Record* 51 (June 1970):462-67.

Citizens Conference on State Legislatures. *The Sometime Governments: A Critical Study of the 50 American Legislatures.* New York: Bantam, 1971.

———. *State Legislatures: An Evaluation of Their Effectiveness.* New York: Praeger, 1971.

Cohn, Rubin G. "The Process of Legislation." *University of Illinois Law Forum,* 1963, no. 1:27-51.

Duncan, Michael P. "Functioning of Illinois House Committee System." Illinois Legislative Council. File 5-528 (March 30, 1965).

Dunn, Charles W., and Samuel K. Gove. "Legislative Reform Vacuum." *National Civic Review* 61 (1972):441-46.

Garvey, Neil F. *The Government and Administration of Illinois.* New York: Thomas Y. Crowell, 1958.

Gove, Samuel K. "Policy Implications of Legislative Reorganization in Illinois." In *State Legislative Innovation: Case Studies of Washington, Ohio, Florida, Illinois, Wisconsin, and California,* edited by James A. Robinson. New York: Praeger, 1973.

———, and Gilbert Y. Steiner. *The Illinois Legislative Process.* Urbana: Institute of Government and Public Affairs, University of Illinois, 1954.

Guild, Frederic H. "Behavioral Patterns for Handling the Legislative Workload." Public Affairs Research Bureau, Southern Illinois University, Carbondale, 1968.

———. "Co-Sponsorship of Bills in the Illinois Legislature." *Public Affairs Bulletin.* Public Affairs Research Bureau, Southern Illinois University, Carbondale (March-April 1971).

———. "Illinois Adopts Legislative Time Scheme: How the New 1967 Rules Worked." *Public Affairs Bulletin.* Public Affairs Research

Bureau, Southern Illinois University, Carbondale (March-April 1968).

————. "In the Second House: A Statistical Analysis of the Operation of the Bicameral System, Illinois Sessions, 1965 and 1967." Occasional Paper, Public Affairs Research Bureau, Southern Illinois University, Carbondale, February 1970.

Hull, Richard M. "Changes Affecting the Introduction of Bills in the Illinois General Assembly." *Illinois Bar Journal* 57 (September 1968) :34-40.

Illinois. General Assembly. Commission on the Organization of the General Assembly. *Improving the State Legislature.* Urbana: University of Illinois Press, 1967.

Katz, Harold A. "The Illinois Experience in Legislative Modernization." In *Strengthening the States: Essays in Legislative Reform,* edited by Donald Herzberg and Alan Rosenthal. New York: Doubleday, 1971.

Kenney, David. *Basic Illinois Government: A Systematic Explanation,* rev. ed. Carbondale: Southern Illinois University Press, 1974.

Lambrecht, William. "Story of a Law: How Assembly Worked Out an Energy Program." *Illinois Issues* 1 (January 1975) :24-26.

Moeller, Stephen. "The Katz Commission: A Study of Legislative Reorganization." Honors thesis, University of Illinois, Urbana, 1967.

Nichols, George A. "The Lawyer as a Draftsman." *University of Illinois Law Forum* 1963, no. 1 :1-15.

Ogilvie, Richard B. "From the Governor's Chair. . . ." In *Strengthening the States,* edited by Donald Herzberg and Alan Rosenthal. New York: Doubleday, 1971.

Voting and Representation

Andrews, James H. "Illinois' At-Large Vote." *National Civic Review* 55 (1966) :253-57.

Barker, Twiley W., Jr. "Illinois Tries Again." *National Civic Review* 54 (1965) :417-21.

————. "A Long, Long Ballot." *National Civic Review* 53 (1964) :170-75.

Blair, George S. *Cumulative Voting: An Effective Electoral Device in Illinois Politics.* Urbana: University of Illinois Press, 1960.

————. "The Case for Cumulative Voting in Illinois." *Northwestern University Law Review* 47 (1952) :344-57.

————. "Cumulative Voting: Patterns of Party Allegiance and Rational Choice in Illinois State Legislative Contests." *American Political Science Review* 52 (1958) :123-30.

Bogert, George T., and William S. Singer. "Legislative Apportionment in Illinois: Mandate and Opportunity." *Chicago Bar Record* 49 (June 1968) :378-84.

Dunn, Charles W. "Cumulative Voting Problems in Illinois Legislative Elections." *Harvard Journal on Legislation* 9 (1972) :627-65.

Gove, Samuel K. "Reapportionment and Illinois Public Policy." *Illinois Business Review* 23 (March 1966) :6-8.

————. *Reapportionment and the Cities: The Impact of Reapportionment on Urban Legislation in Illinois.* Chicago: Center for Research in Urban Government, Loyola University, June 1968.

Hall, Leland E. "The Impact of Electoral Deadlock: New Members and the 1965 Session of the Illinois House." Ph.D. dissertation, University of Illinois, Urbana, 1969.

Hyneman, Charles S., and Julian D. Morgan. "Cumulative Voting in Illinois." *Illinois Law Review* 32 (May 1937) :12-31.

Kenney, David. "Representation in the General Assembly." In *Con-Con: Issues for the Illinois Constitutional Convention,* edited by Samuel K. Gove and Victoria Ranney. Urbana: University of Illinois Press, 1970.

McDowell, James L. *The Politics of Reapportionment in Illinois.* Carbondale: Southern Illinois University Press, 1967.

————. "Changes in the Apportionment System: The Illinois General Assembly 1963-1967." Ph.D. dissertation, University of Illinois, Urbana, 1972.

Moore, Blaine F. *The History of Cumulative Voting and Minority Representation in Illinois, 1870-1919.* Urbana: University of Illinois Press, 1919.

Sawyer, Jack, and Duncan MacRae, Jr. "Game Theory and Cumulative Voting in Illinois: 1920-1954." *American Political Science Review* 56 (1962) :936-46.

Silva, Ruth C. "Relation of Representation and the Party System to the Number of Seats Apportioned to a Legislative District." *Western Political Quarterly* 17 (1964) :742-69.

The 1970 Illinois Constitution

Baum, David C. "A Tentative Survey of Illinois Home Rule (Part I): Powers and Limitations." *University of Illinois Law Forum* 1972, no. 1:137-57.

————. "A Tentative Survey of Illinois Home Rule (Part II) : Legislative Control, Transition Problems, and Intergovernmental Conflict." *University of Illinois Law Forum* 1972, no. 3:559-88.

Braden, George D., and Rubin G. Cohn. *The Illinois Constitution: An Annotated and Comparative Analysis.* Urbana: Institute of Government and Public Affairs, University of Illinois, 1969.

Cole, Stephanie. "Home Rule in Illinois: No. 3. General Assembly Action." *Illinois Issues* 1 (July 1975) :204-7.

Dunn, Charles W. "The Future of Legislative Reform in Illinois: The 1970 Constitution." *Chicago Bar Record* 52 (March 1971) :291-302.

Gove, Samuel K., and Richard J. Carlson. "The Legislature." In *Con-Con: Issues for the Illinois Constitutional Convention,* edited by Samuel K. Gove and Victoria Ranney. Urbana: University of Illinois Press, 1970.

Green, Eugene. "Home Rule, Preemption, and the Illinois General Assembly." In *Home Rule in Illinois,* Final Report, Background Papers, and Speeches, Assembly on Home Rule in Illinois, edited by Stephanie Cole and Samuel K. Gove. Urbana: Institute of Government and Public Affairs, University of Illinois, 1973.

Hanley, William S. "The 1970 Illinois Constitution and the Executive Veto." *Public Affairs Bulletin.* Public Affairs Research Bureau, Southern Illinois University, Carbondale (January-April 1972).

Illinois. Sixth Constitutional Convention. *Record of Proceedings, Committee Proposals — Member Proposals.* Springfield, 1972. Committee on Legislative Article Majority and Minority Proposals. VI:1293-1566.

————. "Legislative Committee Report: An Appendix; Legislative Article: Comparative Information" (May 4, 1970).

Kustra, Robert. "The Formulation of Constitutional Home Rule in Illinois." Ph.D. dissertation, University of Illinois, Urbana, 1975.

Lousin, Ann. "The General Assembly and the 1970 Constitution." *Illinois Issues* 1 (May 1975) :131-34.

Parties and Politics

Derge, David R. "Metropolitan and Outstate Alignments in Illinois and Missouri Legislative Delegations." *American Political Science Review* 52 (1958) :1051-65. Reply: Richard T. Frost, 53 (1959) : 792-95; Rejoinder: 53 (1959) :1078-95.

————. "The Power Position of the Cook County Delegation in the Illinois General Assembly, 1949-1953, as Tested by Roll-Call Votes and Committee Positions." Ph.D. dissertation, Northwestern University, Evanston, Ill., 1955.

Heinz, John P., Robert W. Gettleman, and Morris A. Seeskin. "Legislative Politics and the Criminal Law." *Northwestern University Law Review* 64 (1969):277-358.

Heinecke, Burnell. "New Force in Senate — They Call Themselves 'The Crazy 8.'" *Illinois Issues* 2 (January 1976):21-23.

Keefe, William J. "Party Government and Lawmaking in Illinois General Assembly." *Northwestern University Law Review* 47 (1952): 55-71.

Littlewood, Thomas B. *Bipartisan Coalition in Illinois*. Eagleton Institute, Cases in Practical Politics, no. 22 (McGraw-Hill, 1960).

McGriggs, Lee. "Black Legislative Politics in Illinois: A Theoretical and Structural Analysis." Ph.D. dissertation, University of Illinois, Urbana, 1975.

Martin, John B. "What Those Politicians Do to You." *Saturday Evening Post* 226 (December 12, 19, 26, 1953).

Pensoneau, Taylor. "Walker, Ogilvie, and Kerner Used Different Techniques in Dealing with Legislature." *Illinois Issues* 1 (February 1975):51-53.

Ranney, Austin. *Illinois Politics*. New York: New York University Press, 1960.

Steiner, Gilbert Y. "Legislative Power Blocs," *Illinois Government* no. 18. Institute of Government and Public Affairs, University of Illinois, Urbana, 1963.

————, and Samuel K. Gove. *Legislative Politics in Illinois*. Urbana: University of Illinois Press, 1960.

Toussaint, George W. "Shifting Majorities in the Illinois Senate, 1955-61." Master's thesis, University of Iowa, Iowa City, 1963.

Williams, Jean. "Is Politics 'for Men Only'? How Women Lawmakers React." *Illinois Issues* 1 (June 1975):163-65.

Pressure Groups and Lobbies

Andrews, James H. *Private Groups in Illinois Government*. Urbana: Institute of Government and Public Affairs, University of Illinois, 1965.

Gove, Samuel K. "The Business of the Legislature." *University of Illinois Law Forum* 1963, no. 1:52-71.

Hedlund, Ronald D., and Samuel C. Patterson. "Personal Attitudes, Political Orientation, and Occupational Perspectives of Lobbyists:

The Case of Illinois." *Iowa Business Digest* 37 (November 1966) : 3-10.

Hoffman, George C. "The Lawyer as a Lobbyist." *University of Illinois Law Forum* 1963, no. 1 : 16-26.

Simon, Paul, as told to Alfred Balk. "The Illinois Legislature: A Study in Corruption." *Harper's Magazine* 229 (September 1964) :74-78.

Taxing and Spending

Anton, Thomas J. *The Politics of State Expenditure in Illinois*. Urbana: University of Illinois Press, 1966.

Fisher, Glenn W. *Financing Illinois Government*. Urbana: University of Illinois Press, 1960.

———. *Taxes and Politics: A Study of Illinois Public Finance*. Urbana: University of Illinois Press, 1969.

———, ed. *Illinois State and Local Finance,* Final Report and Background Papers, Assembly on Illinois State and Local Finance. Urbana: Institute of Government and Public Affairs, University of Illinois, 1969.

Fishbane, Joyce D., and Glenn W. Fisher. *Politics of the Purse: Revenue and Finance in the Sixth Illinois Constitutional Convention*. Urbana: University of Illinois Press, 1969.

Kane, Douglas N. "Regional Distribution of Taxes and Expenditures in Illinois." Ph.D. dissertation, University of Illinois, Urbana, 1973.

Serafin, Thom M. "A Watchful Eye on State Accounts: Auditor General Robert Cronson." *Illinois Issues* 1 (November 1975) :332-34.

Press Coverage

Hatch, Richard A. "Reporters and Legislators in Illinois: Their Roles and How They Interact." Ph.D. dissertation, University of Illinois, Urbana, 1969.

Kane, Douglas N. "Newspaper Portraits of the Illinois General Assembly." Master's thesis, University of Illinois, Urbana, 1967.

Littlewood, Thomas B. "The Trials of State House Journalism." *Saturday Review* 49 (December 10, 1966) :82-83.

———. "What's Wrong with Statehouse Coverage." *Columbia Journalism Review* 6 (March-April 1972) :39-45.

Sigale, Merwin K. "Press Coverage of the Illinois Legislature." Master's thesis, University of Illinois, Urbana, 1960.

Weber, Jessica C. "State House Reporters: Their Unofficial Role in the Governmental Process." *Illinois Issues* 1 (April 1975) :118-21.

Index

Adjournment, 25, 26, 33-34; by governor, 29; in Congress, 105
Administration. *See* Governor; State agencies
Administrative agencies. *See* State agencies
Administrative Office of the Illinois Courts, 48
Advisory referenda, 20
Aging, Council on, 99
Aging, Department of, 99
Amendatory vetoes. *See* Vetoes, amendatory
"Amendment by reference," 43
Amendments: in second house, 42n, 58n; on daily calendar, 52; time required for, 57-58n; recommended by committee, 57, 58, 89, 91, 93, 103; voting on, 58; copying of, 58n; and three-reading requirement, 58n. *See also* Constitutional amendments
Annual sessions, 25, 26, 27, 162n
Apportionment. *See* Reapportionment
Appropriation bills, 3, 11-13, 42-43, 44-45; and committees, 12-13, 96; timing of, 30, 44; tabling of, 30, 57; as temporary part of statutes, 41n; on daily calendar, 52; item vetoes of, 65-66; effective dates of, 74; and legislative workload, 98n
Appropriations: for local governments, 12; and majority party task forces, 13; annual, 27. *See also* Budget, state; Governor and state budget
Appropriations Committee, 13, 45n, 80, 88, 91; hearing of bills by, 56; schedule of, 85-86; staffing of, 101

Appropriations process, 101-2, 172-73; in Congress, 44-45n
Archives, State, 94
Assignment of Bills, Committee on, 55, 81, 85, 139
Associated Press, 131, 132
At-large election of 1964, 24n, 153
Auditor general, 13-14
Audits, Department of, 13

Balance of powers. *See* Executive-legislative balance of powers
Banking statutes, 19
Baum, David C., 8
Bills, 42, 53, 62, 85n, 160; enacting clause of, 2, 42; introduction of, 3, 29-31, 41, 43n, 86, 162n; amendatory, 3, 43; emergency, 26n, 29, 45, 74; timing of, 27-28, 167; subjects of, 34, 42-43, 159, 164; prefiling of, 38, 54; identification of, 41, 73; final action on, 42n, 74-75; calling of, 57; and the governor, 72-73; advancement of without reference to committee, 86, 87-88; referral of to committee, 86, 91, 92-93, 94; assignment of, 139-40; explanations of, 168-69. *See also* Companion bills; Deadlines; Effective date
Board of Trustees of the General Assembly Retirement System, 99
Bond authorizations, 10-11
Bond v. Floyd, 16n
Budget, state, 101-2; consideration of, 26, 27; submission date of, 86. *See also* Appropriations; Governor and state budget

Of related interest . . .

STUDIES IN ILLINOIS CONSTITUTION MAKING
Joseph P. Pisciotte, Editor

All books in the series are in paperback @ $3.45 each.